Nonviolent Self-Defense

(#ADNcat)

in 100 messages and an incredible story

MONTABER

Nonviolent Self-Defense

(#ADNcat)

in 100 messages and an incredible story

Martí Olivella i Solé

Published on January 30, 2023 in commemoration
of the 75th anniversary of the assassination of M. Gandhi

MONTABER

Collection: Crítica y ensayo
Publishing director: David Soler

Original title in Catalan: *AutoDefensa Noviolenta (#ADNcat) en 100 missatges i una història increíble.* ISBN: 978-84-19109-37-8

Nonviolent Self–Defense (#ADNcat)
in 100 messages and an incredible story
1st edition, July 2023

© 2023, Martí Olivella Solé
© Illustrations: Joan Lluch, objector and draughtsman
© of this edition: ICG Marge, SL
© Translation: Novact

Publisher: Montaber – Marge Books
Brutau, 160, 1st D – 08203 Sabadell (Barcelona)
Tel. 931 429 486 – montaber@montaber.es
www.montaber.es

Edition: Mercedes Lara
Printed by: Prodigitalk, SL (Martorell, Barcelona)

Paper edition ISBN: 978-84-19109-60-6
Digital edition ISBN: 978-84-19109-61-3
Legal Deposit: B 13963-2023

"Satyagraha is, in the literal sense, adherence to the truth and means, by extension, the force of truth (...) and excludes the use of violence, because man is incapable of knowing the absolute truth and, therefore, does not have the power to punish".

M. GANDHI, 1921.

This edition has been possible thanks to the people who have made a fiscal objection on 2022 and have destined their contributions to the Nonviolent Civil Defense project. The net income from the distribution of the book will also go to continue this project.

Formats

This text is presented in different formats:

Telegram, from December 3, 2022 daily publication of 500 characters in a channel with the possibility to make comments; with key links to books, campaigns, websites...

Mastodont.cat, in the account https://mastodont.cat/@adn of 500 characters (same as Telegram).

The web format, in the blog https://aturemlesguerres.cat/adn-autodefensa-noviolenta/

The electronic book format, in PDF and e.reader.

The paper format, the text and also a summary of the contents of the links to websites, campaigns, books... with illustrations that accompany the different parts of the book.

The author

Martí Olivella i Solé (Barcelona, 1955) was a member of the first group of conscientious objectors to military service (1975-1977 in Franco's Spain) where he learned, in practice, the key elements of nonviolent struggle, together with Pepe Beunza. He spent 5 months in the Castell de Sant Ferran prison (Figueres). The movement of objectors achieved the recognition of the right to object to military service, in the new constitution of 1977. And, thanks to a million of objectors and 50.000 unsubmissive people, in 2001 the compulsory military service was abolished, as a first step towards a world without army and wars.

However, as part of the causes of the wars are due to the political and economic system, he became interested, thanks to Lluís Maria Xirinacs, in the elaboration of alternative models of society around Agustí Chalaux, in the 'Centre d'Estudis Joan Bardina' and, later, in "Ecoconcern - Innovació Social". It was in the association 'Nova - Innovació' where he took up the proposals for alternatives to armed forces: with the "Marxes per la cultura de la pau", with his story *El Planeta del Foc*, with the project to turn jails into Peace Museums 'Castell per la Pau' and with projects of support to nonviolent movements in Iraq, Palestine, Lebanon... And finally, from NOVACT – International Institute for Nonviolence – this support has been given to the nonviolent movements of the southern shore of the Mediterranean.

Since the beginning of the process towards Catalan independence, he has been offering training from 'En peu de pau', and later from 'www.lluitanoviolenta.cat'.

He has actively participated in the collective group "Pau i Treva" and the "Seminari Estat de Pau", promoting the publications by the 'ICIP - Institut Català Internacional per la Pau', of several reference works on alternatives to armed forces: *Construir un estat segur i en pau*, *La Defensa Civil Noviolenta* (Gene Sharp), *Serveis Civils de Pau* (Ruben Campos) or *El Antigolpe* (Gonzalo Arias).

Contents

Note to the versions translated from Catalan

This book arises in Catalan at a specific time and place, in an attempt to respond to several major challenges.

It arises at the end of 2022, that is, under the social impact of the armed conflict in Ukraine and as a "weapon" of the campaign www.aturemlesguerres.cat; it also arises in Catalonia (Spain, Europe), a small country that is experiencing an impasse in its independence process; and, all this, in the context of a growing collapse of civilization, in which the various social movements have difficulty in structuring an eco-social transition, or a transformative nonviolent rebellion at the height of the seriousness of the moment.

The concrete challenges derive from the situation itself:

- What to do when one state invades another?
- What kind of legitimate and non-counterproductive defense should be prepared?
- How to achieve independence without resorting to an armed uprising?
- In a new state, how to create a deterrent and effective defense system without relying on armed forces?
- How to articulate a grassroots movement to defend the territory and its people from the aggressions they may suffer?
- How to strengthen the coherence between eco-feminism and alternatives to militarism and wars?

The answers offered are inspired by nonviolent struggles and resistances of the 20th century, and must be understood in this context. Some of them may even be useful in other contexts. Although some of the situations – for example, the independence process in Catalonia – may not be shared by all readers, the ideas provided may transcend this case, and can be applied to other similar conflicts.

ADNCat (in Catalan, is acronym of AutoDefensa Noviolenta Catalana). ADN is the same acronym of DNA in English.

Choral preface

I would like to thank my friends **Pepe Beunza**, **Llúcia Oliva, Xavier Masllorens**, **Thais Bonilla** and **Raül Romeva** for the comments attached as a plural prologue.

Disarmament, now!

Pepe Beunza Vázquez
Condemned in two court-martial

At my first War Council I tried to explain, although they would not let me, that from the time when Cain killed Abel with an ace mace, according to the Bible, to the atomic bomb and modern chemical and biological weapons, there has been a negative evolution of humanity in which I did not want to participate and, for this reason, I declared myself a conscientious objector to military service. More than fifty years later we continue with the same theme as preachers in the desert, given the current situation, with very small victories, although, in these issues, all are important.

A high-ranking Russian military officer explained on television that we have accumulated bombs to destroy more than a thousand times all trace of life on earth, and an American military proudly showed a missile with the destructive capacity of 60% of all the bombs dropped in the Second World War.

In this situation, it is incomprehensible that disarmament is not a priority proposal on the agenda of politicians, philosophers, religious people, economists or anyone who thinks they are somewhat self-confident, including the military, who know that they cannot defend themselves when the powder explodes.

That is why this book is so important. The paranoia of legitimate defense has turned this principle into an excuse for the big business of the military industrial political complex and when they organize a war like the one in Ukraine, all western politicians become warriors filling the coffers of the arms manufacturers, oil companies and friends. If we spend it all on the army, wars are inevitable.

We have the right and the duty to defend ourselves from invasion or injustice, but we must do so intelligently, effectively and ethically. Wars are a crime against humanity. We know this for a fact. Therefore, learning to defend ourselves, as this book explains, is a path to the survival of the human species. Putin will say it very clearly, if he gives up the nuclear weapon, it will all be over.

Nonviolent Self-Defense can deliver us from this bad dream. For the moment we are still alive by miracle. We must take advantage of it.

Peace is in our hands

Llúcia Oliva

Journalist, former correspondent in Washington and Moscow

My mother is 97 years old, and when she hears a dog howling, she still gets upset because it reminds her of the Spanish war of 1936-39 that she lived through when she was a little girl. She suffered first the rearguard and then the front and she has kept it all in her aching heart for almost a century.

Her father in prison, the pain she went through, the assassinations she witnessed, the bombings she had to protect herself from at the age of twelve, the fear that her big sister would be raped, the helplessness of seeing her godfather agonizing without medical help, the desolation in the face of the hordes of refugees escaping day and night at the end of the war, the machine gun that the soldiers installed on the roof of her house that made the walls crumble and the ceilings fall, the last resisters, the young boys shot by the bullets and lying in the fields. And then, the hatred between the old enemies of war...

My mother has not forgotten any of that, but she also remembers the neighbor who used to run through the woods at night to bring her a little bit of food; the neighbor who accompanied her to rescue her father from prison; the friend who helped her to protect herself from the bombs that were falling on the Barceloneta beach. Small gestures of solidarity and affection in the midst of that hell!

A war never ends when the fighting is over and its physical and psychological consequences mark forever the people who have lived through it and even their descendants. Our mother taught us to never throw away a piece of bread, but also that wars do not solve conflicts, that the pain they cause is greater than the victory of some over others.

This is the origin of my desire that peace and agreement should be imposed when as a journalist I cover a conflict, any conflict. Hence my conviction that we journalists must be committed to peace, as we are committed to freedom, human rights and against gender violence.

When I was a correspondent in Moscow, during the time of Mikhail Gorbatxev, I witnessed how the opportunity for a better and more peaceful world was lost. The then top Soviet leader proposed to other world leaders to resolve conflicts through international cooperation. Unfortunately, he lacked the power to impose the idea and the heads of the other powers did not listen to him.

Thus, the task of achieving a better and more peaceful world is in the hands of the citizens. As this tireless pacifist Martí Olivella says, if oppression and injustice are maintained it is because we collaborate with them. For this reason, in his book "Nonviolent Self-Defense", Olivella gives people the tools so that, in case of conflict, they can maintain their dignity and work for peace so that waging war does not cost those who have provoked it.

An unprecedented but not impossible utopia

XAVIER MASLLORENS I ESCUBÓS

President of l'ICIP (Institut Català Internacional per la Pau)

Nonviolent action has very little propaganda. Indeed, the action of nonviolent resistance –or disobedience–, especially violates the nuclei of power in all societies, be they democratic, authoritarian or dictatorial. Although these actions are deeply respectful of the *status quo* (they accept the punishment of the laws that they precisely want to change or repeal), they are deeply uncomfortable due to their own nature of denial of what they consider unjust.

The Spanish State is no exception, despite the fact that the Supreme Court admitted twenty years ago that nonviolent civil disobedience is a legal form of demonstration and opposition. We have, moreover, examples of success of these actions, when they are transformed into strategies designed and carried out in a collective and coordinated manner. Perhaps the most recent examples are the objection to compulsory military service and the insubmission to civilian service as a substitute for military service.

But this book goes beyond that. If all this provokes hives in the apparatuses of the State, imagine the discomfort that must be provoked –even in a large part of the citizenry– by an alternative security proposal that does not involve extermination, coercion and armament, but rather a powerful and organized force of nonviolent civil defense.

In the following pages, information and proposals –in the form of small pills– that aim to achieve the creation of a non-violent self-defense force, in a new security paradigm are presented. An unprecedented but not impossible utopia, contrary to the secular model promoted by the States of an armed defense that provokes more and more insecurity. You will find a good way to dream that humanity can solve conflicts in a different, cooperative and supportive way if it is prepared consciously and wins public opinion. And you will also find elements of thought to prepare individually and collectively. Because, as you will read, "when a war breaks out it is too late to organize a non-violent civil defense".

What we do not know, seems impossible

Thais Bonilla Martínez

Responsible, in Novact Institute of Nonviolence, for the support to human rights defenders and member of the Advisory Council of the Guillem Agulló School

What we do not know is impossible. For this reason, the dissemination and teaching of the principles and strategy of Nonviolence have always been a priority objective for Martí Olivella, as well as other people convinced that there is a way without weapons, armies of war, or violence.

Nonviolent self-defense is a transformative power that is not only a defensive tool of resistance and a way to resolve injustices. It works as a trigger for a more equitable and inclusive alternative to the world we live in: it generates a sense of community, helps to reduce social imbalances, focuses on the causes of oppression and amplifies popular power.

In today's times, information flows fast. Short and direct messages that say it all. In adaptation to this world of social networks and digital platforms, the present publication breaks down in detail everything that lies behind a civil system of nonviolent defense in 100 short messages, elaborated in some cases as a question and answer and a story in the form of narrative fiction. It approaches, offering various resources for consultation, the challenges, the realities, the consequences and the necessary personal and social preparation for this approach. "In the case of civil defense, the whole society becomes a force for nonviolent struggle," it says.

Moreover, it gives examples. He shows us those practices that have made it possible, but that have been erased from history because they do not serve as a dream of something different. So that they are no longer hope. The writing talks about the Czechoslovakia of 1968, the Denmark of the Second World War, the Lithuania of 1991 and 2015, the experience of the Indigenous Guard of Cauca in Colombia since the year 2000 or the challenges of Gandhi's India in 1922.

And now, he leaves us the challenge: "In times of peace is when you have to prepare and organize yourself".

Are we willing to *cooperate to face incredible challenges?*

Yes, it is possible

RAÜL ROMEVA I RUEDA
Economist, doctor in international relations, doctor in education and sport sciences.

Is it possible to respond to violence with nonviolence? The answer to this question is yes, without a doubt. We have plenty of examples, of all kinds and conditions.

If anyone is not yet convinced, I recommend you read the numerous contributions of someone who is considered one of the greatest exponents of the strategy of nonviolence: Gene Sharp, professor at Massachusetts and Harvard, and founder of the Albert Einstein Institution.

In *Civilian-based defense*, a book published in catalan by the Institut Català Internacional per la Pau in 2018, Sharp develops two theses. On the one hand, that it is possible to develop civilian policies and methods of nonviolent civil defense against internal state and external aggressions, and, on the other hand, that dictatorships and oppressions can be avoided with the ability to oppose an energetic and effective nonviolent struggle.

In the foreword to the aforementioned book, Martí Olivella emphasizes that in the Baltic countries –Lithuania, Latvia and Estonia– independence was declared in 1990 and had to face an attempt of aggression by the Soviet authorities in January 1991, who wanted to regain control. During this crisis, the three governments relied heavily on the methods of nonviolent resistance they had learned from the writings of Gene Sharp.

The Lithuanian Minister of Defense, Andreus Butkevicius, in 1991 said: "We will never have a strong enough army to defend ourselves against a foreign aggressor. Our objective can only be to defeat him morally, economically and politically, not physically." And commenting on Gene Sharp's book, he proclaimed, "I'd rather have this book than an atomic bomb,"

For all these reasons, I consider that this is a very valuable document to face the convulsive times we are living in, and that it helps a lot, with ideas and arguments, to create a base for a peaceful and democratic movement, as is already being , thanks to significant initiatives.

Besides the aforementioned work by Gene Sharp, I would also like to recommend another book of great validity and contrasted solvency; undoubtedly, one of the best materials we have at our disposal today. I am talking about *How to make the revolution*, by Srdja Popovic.

Popovic proposes that action must follow, above all, three very logical steps. First step: preach nonviolence within the movement. Second step: train fellow activists so that they know how to recognize the possible sources of friction. And third step: in order to shore up the movement against the temptations of the violence demon, it is necessary to defend it from the provocateurs who, inevitably, will try to sneak into the party.

All three steps are perfectly applicable to our case. In fact, I claim that this is the case and I commit myself to be a practitioner and a leader.

The text that Martí Olivella offers us now, in the form of short stories, almost aphorisms, is part of this tradition, and points out a path that is both necessary and useful.

And the fact is that our commitment to nonviolence is not only a matter of principle, but also for more pragmatic reasons.

In *Why Civil Resistance Works: The Strategic Logic of NonViolent Conflict,* Erica Chenoweth and Maria J. Stephan study all conflicts between 1900 and 2006, 323 in total. The result is clear: take up arms and you have a 26% chance of success; practice the principles of nonviolence and the percentage rises to 53%.

If you do not believe in the principles, trust at least in statistics.

Introduction

Laying the foundations of a **civilian system of nonviolent defense** is one of the objectives of the commitment of the campaign www.aturemlesguerres.cat launched on November 2, 2022. We hope that these messages, and the dialogue they provoke, will help us to imagine how we can organize it. You are invited to comment, give examples, raise questions and suggest illustrative images. Let's start! #ADNcat

Stop Wars Campaing (Campanya Aturem les guerres)

Since November 2, 2022 we are arriving every day, one or more days a week... more than 350 people in 12 cities, in front of city halls (Barcelona, Girona, Sabadell, Terrassa, Banyoles, Sentmenat, Oliana, Figueres, Gràcia BCN, Manresa...) in squares (Vilanova i la Geltrú), in front of the Delegation of the Treasury (Lleida) and

www.aturemlesguerres.cat

in front of the 2 delegations of the Ministry of War (Barcelona and Tarragona), all presenting petitions of motions in favor of the Initiative for Peace.

How to organize Nonviolent Self-Defense in 100 messages and an incredible story

This book is written in the form of short messages. While we prepare the edition, we publish it on the Telegram channel and group https://t.me/ADN_AutoDefensaNoviolenta. We also publish it on Mastodon https://mastodont.cat/@adn with the hashtag #ADNcat as an alternative to Twitter that we do not want to use as an act of boycott to these networks and especially to the self-serving policies of its new owner.

As you will see throughout the text, Nonviolent Self-Defense (ADN in its acronym in Catalan) is a new concept that I use to refer in an abbreviated way both to a Civil Nonviolent

Self-Defense System and to its concretization in an organization, that allows us to start building, here and now, a proposal specifically exposed in the 3rd part of the book.

For more information, to make comments or to offer collaborations: info@lluitanoviolenta.cat.

https://lluitanoviolenta.cat/projecte-defensa-noviolenta

https://aturemlesguerres.cat/adn-autodefensa-noviolenta/

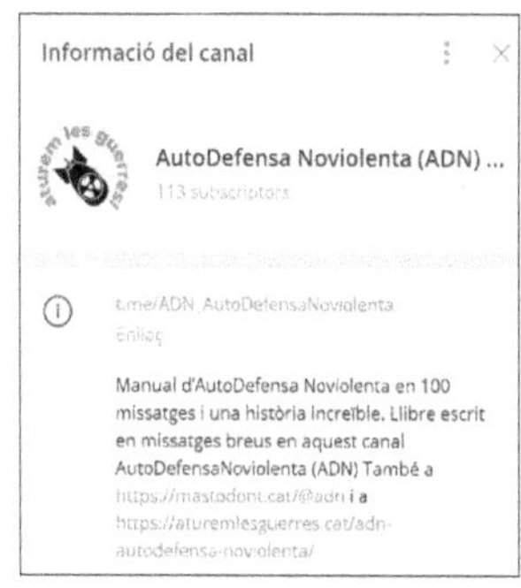

https://t.me/ADN_
AutoDefensaNoviolenta

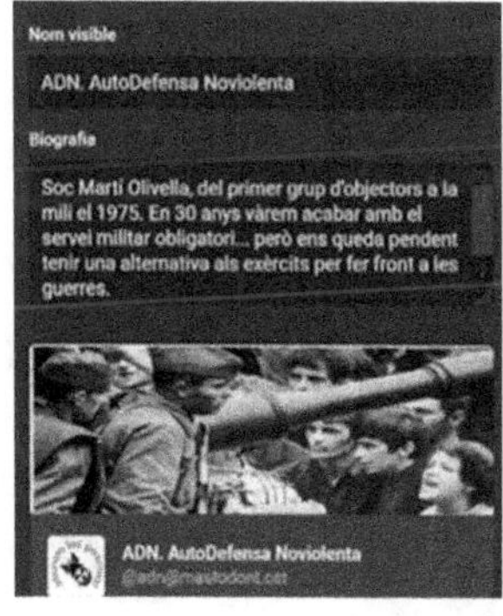

https://mastodont.cat/@adn

Part 1

FREQUENTLY ASKED QUESTIONS WITH SURPRISING ANSWERS

1. Only by saying 'No to war', can we stop War?

Any balanced person is against wars. We can't solve conflicts by putting more fuel in the fire. How can we vindicate rights and freedoms or modify borders while destroying, wounding, torturing, killing, raping people, civilians or military? We say no to wars but, if someone attacks us, what should we do in a world with more than 30 wars, with thousands of deaths? when so many people suffer them directly or suffer them indirectly? #ADNcat

2. Don't we have the right to defend ourselves when we are attacked?

What to do when we are attacked, invaded, occupied? We have to defend ourselves! But, how to do it without provoking more violence? How to make an effective defense, which does not provoke more destruction and death than it intends to avoid? We have the right and the duty to defend the lives of people, of peoples and their organizations, of nature and the Earth; to defend ourselves from all kinds of aggressions, social, economic, political, cultural... also military. #ADNcat

3. If we say **No** to war, what do we say **Yes** to?

We say NO to wars, to the arms race, to the growing militarization, to military pacts... We say yes to multilateral organizations, to disarmament, to international law... but also, and so far it has not been done, to civilian systems of nonviolent self-defense! Self-defense cannot be the excuse to start or escalate any war, which causes the opposite effect to the expected one: it does not protect the population, nor its rights, nor its assets. #ADNcat

4. How to defend ourselves without provoking more war?

How can we organize an effective defense that reduces death and destruction? Almost always people identify "defense" with "armed defense" and we do not know how to defend ourselves without resorting to armies and their lethal weapons. But, as we will see, spontaneously some people have known how to defend themselves without opposing armed resistance to very powerful invading troops. #ADNcat

5. What have these "nonviolent civil defenses" taught us?

When the people stand up to the invaders without violence, show the soldiers the lies with which they have been mobilized, object to and obstruct the invasion, do not cooperate in anything and disobey the orders... the invasion is shuddering. In the best-known cases, the Nazi occupation of Denmark 1940 or the invasion of Czechoslovakia 1968, the destruction was reduced, the motivation of the troops was weakened and the expected performance of the occupier reduced. #ADNcat

6. What is the art of nonviolent self-defense?

It is a socially cohesive and balanced population, ready to organize itself and to take a stand to defend its life and its country without relying on the armed forces as the means of its security and protection. If well organized, it will mean economic, moral and political costs to the invader, to move and maintain an occupying force, and it will be without the arguments of "fighting terrorism" from a people who do not respond with violence! #ADNcat

7. Why nonviolent self-defense can be the best deterrent?

The invader must also know that the occupation will not surrender, due to the radical non-cooperation and disobedience of the people. The best dissuasion is to warn them that the occupation will not pay off. On the other hand, nuclear deterrence does not prevent wars and increases the danger —by accident or by ambush— of provoking an unimaginable holocaust, that is, the absolute failure of the supposed objectives of legitimate defense. #ADNcat

8. Why do spontaneous responses to block tanks, fail?

When war breaks out it is too late to organize a nonviolent civil defense. As we have seen in Ukraine, there can be spontaneous responses of standing up to the tanks. But when there are deaths on both sides, the spiral of violence is not easy to stop and the retaliatory acts are triggered. Now is the time to get organized. In times of peace is when it is time to prepare and organize ourselves (as the armies are always doing). #ADNcat

9. Why haven't states organized nonviolent civil defense?

The states have the monopoly of violence and they exercise it with the armies. Some more democratic ones organize the population in civil protection as a complementary system to armed defense. No state with an army has a civil defense alternative to military defense. The people of a country without a state or an army, if they know how to activate a nonviolent self-defense, can facilitate independence and their own defense, once achieved. #ADNcat

10. What are the social conditions favorable to civil defense?

It is easier to defend and protect what we feel as our own or what we esteem. The first condition for making an effort, for putting aside comforts and life, is that we feel we are part of the society in which we live, and that there is enough social cohesion to make it worth defending. Society must not tolerate great imbalances, inequalities or oppressions related to income, consumption, resources, possibilities... Neither among the population itself, nor between the population and the natural environment. #ADNcat

11. Does the defense of the current aggressions prepare for a hypothetical military aggression?

As there is no balanced society, the practice of nonviolent self-defense must be exercised against the aggressions and violence that each territory suffers today, in order to tend to restore the broken balances. This work has two virtues: it improves living conditions, social cohesion and, at the same time, it creates the more favorable conditions to face a hypothetical, and unwanted, armed aggression. #ADNcat

Part 2

WHAT IS NONVIOLENT CIVIL DEFENSE?

12. What are the advantages of nonviolent civil defense?

It offers important short - and long - term strategic advantages over traditional military strategies in the defense of people, governments and territories. It exploits the political vulnerabilities of adversaries when it seeks ways to undermine the essential pillars - economic, political, moral - that sustain the adversary and its war machine, while minimizing the costs, damage and death to the society under attack. #ADNcat

13. What else does nonviolent civil defense bring to the table?

Nonviolent civil defense can instill a significant degree of civic empowerment, self-organization, decentralization and civic solidarity, necessary elements for a post-war democratization. "Civil" not only refers to the fact that it is formed by citizens, people of the people, workers, peasants, indigenous people, etc., but it is a peaceful, unarmed and nonviolent defense, as opposed to a "military" one. #ADNcat

Most of the messages in this 2nd part are inspired by Maciej Bartkowski's article from 2015.

Nonviolent civil defense to counter Russia's hybrid warfare

https://lluitanoviolenta.cat/files/pdf/
gov1501_whitepaper_bartkowski.pdf

Specialized in history, study and practice of civil resistance. He observes how ordinary people organize and exercise constructive and coercive nonviolent resistance to win their freedoms and rights, often against seemingly insurmountable odds. His interests include strategies of nonviolent resistance against dictatorships, national defense and the fight against foreign and national disinformation.

In this article in 2015, he sets out the well-established principles of strategic nonviolent conflict and documents its effectiveness in resisting and rolling back oppression. He goes on to describe how President Vladimir Putin's Russia has found ways to turn this form of struggle to offensive ends, especially in Ukraine, but also in other countries on Russia's periphery. It concludes with some political recommendations on how Ukraine and NATO can resist this aggression using totally or partially nonviolent means.

14. What does the effectiveness of nonviolent civil defense depend on?

It depends on organizational planning, effective partnership between public and civic organizations, as well as with people involved in the application of nonviolent strategies. In contrast to violent armed popular resistance, which is in the hands of a limited number, usually men operating in a clandestine guerrilla network, nonviolent resistance can mobilize and involve the whole of society. #ADNcat

15. The population is the basis of nonviolent civil defense

Everyone can participate in overt or discreet acts of non-cooperation, disobedience and refusal to accept the authority of the repressive or invading adversary. Nonviolent actions of all kinds can mobilize many more thousands, perhaps millions of people than armed resistance ever could, bringing real, powerful and strong power to the defense against the invasion and the resistance against the occupation. #ADNcat

16. What role does the population play in nonviolent civil defense?

The "population" is to be understood as the citizens in general and the organizations of the attacked country, as well as the citizens and organizations of the country of the invading armed force; also the civic networks, and groups of other countries to which, depending on the messages they receive, can have the capacity to give their support, on one side or the other. Nonviolent defense has to seek the support of these three types of population. #ADNcat

17. Lithuanian government manual on nonviolent civil defense

The Lithuanian Ministry of Defense, as we will see in more detail, published in 2015 a manual for the Lithuanian people to use in case of a foreign invasion. It asserts that citizens can resist aggression against their country not only through armed struggle. Civil defense or nonviolent civil resistance is another form of citizen involvement in the face of aggression. #ADNcat

18. **The disconcert in the occupant that is provoked by nonviolent defense.**

The occupation of Denmark and Holland was a great challenge for the German army when the population resorted to nonviolent resistance to defend themselves. The German Nazis were experts in violence and had been trained to confront and defeat opponents who used this method, either with the army or with guerrillas. But other forms of civil and nonviolent forms of resistance were baffling to them. #ADNcat

19. **The occupier justifies his repressive action when the resistance is violent.**

When the Danish resistance was violent the German Nazis were happy because they knew how to act and also when the nonviolent forms were mixed with guerrilla action, because this way they could justify the combination of a drastic and bloody repressive action against both forms of resistance, at the same time violent and nonviolent. #ADNcat

20. The secret of nonviolent civil defense: all for One

In the ideal nonviolent civil defense, the entire population, including its institutions, networks and formal and informal groups, are part of the resistance and defense force. This force, in addition to the deployment of communication strategies and psychological operations, wages a daily war of non-cooperation and disobedience directed against the aggressor in all areas of social, political, economic and cultural life. #ADNcat

21. The secret of nonviolent civil defense: increasing the costs of the invader

Total non-cooperation makes any invasion or subsequent occupation unsustainable in the long run for the attacker. National civil defense is intended to increase the costs to the invader by shaking the loyalty of his troops, his crucial internal supporters and the public at large, while enhancing the internal cohesion, solidarity and self-organization of the defending combatant society. #ADNcat

22. The secret of nonviolent civil defense: political struggle by political means.

In its essential core, the national nonviolent civil defense is a political struggle carried out with political, social, economic, cultural means... Through local and national civilian networks. Flexible but integrated networks that can mobilize hundreds of thousands, or milions, of people to take action against the aggressor in a disciplined, self-organized, agile and flexible nonviolent struggle. #ADNcat

23. Examples of civilian defense against powerful military forces

In the history of violent armed conflicts we are rediscovering frightening and surprising examples of civil defense and nonviolent resistance against militarily more powerful foreign adversaries. The invading adversary, who bases his strength on military violence, prefers to confront the defenders by fighting with lethal weapons where he knows he has a clear advantage over the opponent. #ADNcat

24. Surprising examples of civil defense that baffle invaders

The invader, once challenged with the asymmetric response of mass nonviolent actions of disobedience and non-cooperation, hesitates and has to react improvisedly to the events instead of being able to take the initiative: he loses precious time and resources in having to adjust tactics and strategies to the political and economic battlefield, less favorable and unusual, for the military. #ADNcat

25. The surprising and effective Danish civil resistance to the Nazi invasion

In World War II, the Danes, as mentioned above, launched a campaign of total non-cooperation with the Nazi occupiers. This kind of resistance helped the Danes to realize that they could do something to confront a much stronger and brutal adversary. It also made them more supportive and helped them to create information and communication systems; and to save many lives.

The Danish population went on numerous strikes, "sit-down strike" or "going home early", as well as boycotts, demonstrations and industrial sabotage. These actions were to undermine the expected German economic exploitation of the country. The German army responded with repression and states of emergency, proving that the Danish actions were harming it.

In their struggle against the occupiers, the Danish population was guided by 10 commandments of disobedience:

1. You must not go to work in Germany and Norway.
2. You will do work badly for the Germans
3. You will work slowly for the Germans.
4. You will destroy important machines and machinery [that serve the Germans].
5. Destroy everything that could be of benefit to the Germans.
6. Slow down all transport [used by the Germans].
7. Boycott German and Italian films and newspapers.
8. Do not buy from the Nazi shops.
9. You will treat traitors for what they are worth.
10. Protect any person persecuted by the Germans.

In the course of what we now call a classic civil defense, the Danes spared their country a certain amount of destruction that might otherwise have been similar to the destruction of countries like Poland. In the process of civil resistance, through their solidarity networks, the Danes saved hundreds of thousands of lives, including those of many Jews. #ADNcat

26. The surprising and effective Czechoslovakian resistance to the Soviet troops

The people of Czechoslovakia took nonviolent action against the invasion of the Soviet and Warsaw Pact troops in 1968. As a result of this resistance, the Soviet invasion lasted 8 months instead of the initially planned few days. Czechs and Slovaks denied the aggressor all kinds of services, food, water, housing and information.

They did it with a simple 10-point instruction that was published in the main newspaper. When a Soviet soldier wanted something from the residents they were advised to answer: 1. I don't know. 2. None of your buisness 3. Don't say anything. 4. I don't have it. 5. I don't know how to do it. 6. Don't give them. 7. I can't do anything about it. 8. Don't sell them anything. 9. Don't show them anything. 10. Don't do anything.

Everywhere, the walls of the buildings were covered with hand-painted banners and posters. People everywhere were reading the newspapers and leaflets that were coming out of the clandestine printing presses, despite the efforts of the occupying forces to stop them. It was the image of a city with inhabitants who were absolutely united in a "passive" resistance, unarmed against the alien intruders.

Wherever someone had fallen victim to the Soviet bullets there were improvised monuments with masses of flowers and national flags. The street corner signs had been removed or altered to confuse the occupying forces when they wanted to arrest someone or occupy a building. #ADNcat

27. What can we learn from the Czechoslovakian resistance to the Soviet troops?

This strategy of civil resistance did not expel or defeat the Soviet army, nor did armed resistance. Instead, the strategy of "socially isolating the invaders and denying them the usable use of national resources: personnel, technology and assets" significantly frustrated the Soviets' occupation plans.

The initial plan of the invading troops of the Warsaw Pact was to wrest control of the country from the hands of the reformist communist leaders of Czechoslovakia and establish undisputed Soviet military and political control over the country in 4 days. Nevertheless, it took them 8 months to do it, much longer than would have been the case if the resistance had been violent.

An armed attack of Czechs and Slovaks against the invading Soviets would have ensured a complete and heavy defeat as it happened in Hungary, the previous decade, in November 1956. In Budapest, once the orders were given, the Soviet forces took only 6 days to defeat the Hungarian armed attack.

The nonviolent resistance allowed the Czechoslovaks to preserve the social and economic fabric and to safeguard the civic strength to continue the resistance with nonviolent self-organization and mobilization. This, unknowingly, laid the foundations for the peaceful transition of Czechoslovakia to democracy in 1989, without forgetting the unprecedented peaceful divorce of the Czech Republic and Slovakia in 1993. #ADNcat

28. The oblivion of good experiences and new attempts to open up new paths

Both in Denmark and in Czechoslovakia civil defense protected the civilians and the country better than any armed resistance. Despite these - certainly relative - successes, the idea never gained attraction in the militarized West during the Cold War. However, it had a brief revival immediately after the end of the Cold War, especially in the Baltic Republics in the context of their independence. #ADNcat

29. The bets of the Baltic Republics for civil defense

The Baltic States in 1990, with the experience of the independence process, considered adopting civilian nonviolent strategies in national defense, since they recognized that their conventional military capabilities were insignificant compared to those of Russia and that, should war arrive, occupation would be inevitable. Therefore, these countries drew up plans for the total resistance of the citizens. #ADNcat

30. Lithuania's commitment

After the independence referendum (1991), the Supreme Council of Lithuania regulated the actions of citizens and institutions in the event of Soviet occupation. It demanded adherence "to the principles of disobedience, nonviolent resistance and political and social non-cooperation as the main means of struggle for independence". And a decree established the Commission of Psychological Defense and Civil Resistance to the Department of Defense. #ADNcat

31. Latvia's bet

The Popular Front of Latvia in 1990 called for the civilian population to get involved in total non-cooperation in case of occupation, as well as to "ignore the orders of the attackers, not to participate in any election or referendum, and to document all the crimes perpetrated by the attackers". They prepared plans to defend public institutions, forming chains of unarmed people all around them.

In 1991, the Supreme Council of Latvia agreed on the creation of a Nonviolent Resistance Center: civil defense in Latvia should be a constant complement to its military defenses, in order to compensate for its relative military weakness, improve the self-esteem of its citizens and serve as a possible deterrent in case of a possible aggression.

Civil Defense would be used: 1) as a basic means of defense in case the aggressor army far exceeds that of the Latvian military

https://blogs.lavanguardia.com/berlin-poch/el-kaganato-de-kiev-y-otras-historias-55192

In Lithuania there was a genuine national people's movement. Moscow played games by mobilizing the Russian minority. It wanted to provoke clashes and then intervene militarily as a "mediator". This led to "Bloody Sunday" on January 13, 1991. The Russian troops arrived at the TV tower to dislodge it, but the citizens blocked the place. Then snipers acted. More than a dozen people were killed by gunfire and many more were wounded. They were shot at from the rooftops and balconies of the surrounding buildings. Who shot at the crowd? "My men were not stationed there," "The KGB special troop did not carry live ammunition in their weapons, only in their pockets as a reserve, our goal was to enter the TV headquarters," explains the head of the Russian operation, Mikhail Golovatov (in Die Presse, September 3, 2011). All this was said immediately after the event, but who would have believed that Goliath did not shoot David and that it was not a "KGB massacre"? It was more units, since direct military defense is useless and can even serve as a pretext for violent repressions against civilians; 2) as an additional means of defense, if it is in danger from an aggressor the forces of which are approximately equal to its own; 3) as an additional means of defense in case of a coup d'état. #ADNcat

than ten years before Butkevicius himself explained that it was his men, armed with hunting rifles, who shot at the crowd from the rooftops. He said so in an interview with "Obzor" magazine published in 2000:

"I cannot justify my action to the victims' relatives, but I can justify it to history, because those dead inflicted a double violent blow against two essential bastions of Soviet power: the army and the KGB. That is how we discredited them. I say it clearly: it was I who planned everything that happened. I had worked for quite some time at the Albert Einstein Institution with Professor Gene Sharp, who was then in charge of what was defined as "civil defense," in other words psychological warfare. Yes, I programmed the way to put the Russian army in difficulty, in such an awkward situation that it would force every Russian officer to embarrass himself. It was psychological warfare. In that conflict we had not been able to win with the use of force, that was very clear to us, that is why I moved the battle to another plane, that of psychological confrontation, and I won".

"Otherwise a lot more people would have died, in that situation only those who died, died," Butkevicius says in the January 2013 video.

Author's note: False flag terrorist attacks have nothing to do with non-violent civil defense or psychological warfare, no matter who does it or how they justify it.

32. Estonia's bet

In 1991, Estonian officials devised the "Civil Disobedience" plan which advised the people to: "treat all orders contradicting Estonian law as unlawful; carry out strict disobedience and non-cooperation with all Soviet attempts to enforce control; refuse to supply vital information to the Soviet authorities; and, when necessary, eliminate street names, traffic signs, house numbers, etc... not to be provoked into reckless actions; to document in writing and with film the Soviet actions and to use all channels to distribute this documentation internationally; to preserve the functioning of political and social organizations, e.g. to create security organizations and to store essential equipment; to implement mass actions when appropriate; and to engage in creative communication with potentially hostile forces." #ADNcat

33. How long did the Baltics bets last?

After the failed coup d'état in Moscow in August 1991, Latvia and Estonia abandoned civilian-based national defense. Lithuania was to continue it and in 1996 adopted the Law on National Security: "in case of an assault, citizens and their self-activated structures shall undertake civil protection actions - nonviolent resistance, disobedience and non-collaboration with the illegal administration - as well as armed resistance." #ADNcat

34. NATO will frustrate these bets?

In 2004, Lithuania, along with 2 other Baltic states and 4 Central European countries, joined NATO, creating the perception that the asymmetry between the Lithuanian armed forces and their likely enemy to the east was no longer relevant. In 2005, the civil defense strategy was withdrawn from the Lithuanian national security law. Thus NATO was to kill interest in non-military and nonviolent civil defense strategies in the Baltic States. #ADNcat

35. The return of Lithuania to civil defense?

The Lithuanian Ministry of National Defense, as we have seen, published in 2015 a "Manual on how to prepare for emergency and war situations". It reintroduced nonviolent civil defense in the national defense strategy highlighting the role of state institutions, emergency services, security forces, including measures to increase the security of the population in case of armed conflict.

The Handbook provides details on actions that civilians can take to defy external aggression without weapons. The handbook illustrates the extent to which the Lithuanian government has become skeptical about NATO's ability to deal with the threat of external hybrid warfare. It highlights Gene Sharp's "198 nonviolent methods" with the different categories of tactics: protest and persuasion, non-cooperation and nonviolent intervention.

The Manual, as Sharp stated, affirms that "in the case of civil defense, the whole of society is a force for nonviolent struggle". The manual proposes the use of any of the categories of nonviolent tactics depending on the situation and encourages organized noncooperation, including boycotts and disobedience campaigns in the case of occupation.

The Manual advises to distribute leaflets and clandestine press, to go on "hunger strikes" and "sit-down strikes", not to recognize the occupying institutions and not to participate, to

198 Nonviolent action methods

https://www.aeinstein.org/
198-methods-of-nonviolent-action

Gene Sharp was a North American political scientist and writer, known for his extensive work in defense of nonviolence as a struggle against power. He proposed that nonviolent action, far from being passive, could be "a technique of struggle that involves the use of psychological, social, economic and political power". For him, nonviolent conflict implies "fighting 'battles', it requires a strategy and a set of enlightened tactics, and demands courage, discipline and sacrifice from its 'soldiers'". One of his contributions is his list of "198 methods of nonviolent action" (1973), in which he suggests tactics for movements.

establish a network of web portals that disseminate information about the civil resistance, carry national symbols, stay at home to "welcome" the invaders with empty streets and buildings, ignore the curfew and "do not help the occupiers in any way".

It also recommends training exercises - what might be called nonviolent war games - to prepare and practice the implementation of these measures. According to the Manual, the greater the understanding of nonviolent actions among a general population, the better prepared people are to use them. #ADNcat

36. How to extend the nonviolent battlefield
     to the opponent's population?

In 1923, French and Belgian troops occupied the mining and in-dustrial Ruhr in response to the failure of the Weimar Republic to meet the war reparations agreed at Versailles. The opinions of French and Belgian society on the invasion changed gradually, but significantly, as the effect of the nonviolent stance of the German population of the Ruhr became evident.

Thousands of Frenchmen went to the Ruhr as soldiers or civilians and became advocates for the Germans. For the first time they saw the Germans as they really were. They met a hard-working people, who lived in tenement houses, people very different from what they had been led to believe by the British propaganda. There were many high-ranking officers who were replaced by their friendly attitude towards the Germans. #ADNcat

37. The effectiveness of fraternity
    in the change of leadership

Some Palestinians try to reach out to Israeli activists who oppose
the Israeli government's occupation policies, but their efforts to
win over a section of Israeli society are undermined by the violence of other Palestinian groups. In these cases, the nonviolent
strategy is based on reducing the social distance between the
society that is defending itself and the population living in the
regime that is attacking that society. #ADNcat

38. Civil defense achieves more sympathy
    than violent resistance

Civil defense has a better chance of gaining international sym-
pathy, solidarity and technical and economic aid than violent
resistance. Theoretically, democracies do not always decide to
supply arms to a party of a conflict. Democratic societies often
remain divided on the issue of military aid, even if their governments ultimately approve this assistance.

In contrast, international civil defense assistance can often
mobilize millions of people abroad. For example, the nonviolent struggle against apartheid in South Africa in the 1980s

mobilized and united the North American public around the "Free South Africa" campaign. Despite Reagan's opposition, the campaign led to the adoption of economic sanctions by the US Congress in 1986. #ADNcat

39. The two ways: governmental initiative and citizen's initiative

Many of the historical examples of resistance and civil defense have been improvised in the face of the impossibility of confronting militarily a much superior armed force and with the objective of avoiding the maximum number of deaths, casualties and destruction. The success, always relative and temporary, has been greater when government and population have joined forces to confront the invasion and occupation.

Apart from Lithuania, no European state has bet on Nonviolent Civil Defense, nor seems to be willing to do so, and even less in the framework of NATO, which has destroyed any attempt to apply it, in order to maintain its hegemony, and its dependance on arms and militarism. This would be, the almost non-existent, way of 'governmental initiative of Civil Defense'

Therefore, although nonviolent civil defense, combined governmental-citizen, would seem to be the most effective, when the government does not want to bet on it, there is only the citizen initiative to organize a nonviolent civil defense system. And it would be good to consider, that the implementation of this Nonviolent Civilian way, could arouse again the interest for governmental involvement and generate, thus, a more powerful system of civil and governmental nonviolent defense. #ADNcat

40. Defense in stateless nations

If almost no state with an army is interested in advancing towards a nonviolent civilian defense, only stateless nations without an army have a double opportunity in the civilian way of nonviolent defense: to improve the capabilities of the population to achieve independence and, once achieved, to be able to defend it without having to resort to the slow, costly and perilous creation and maintenance of an armed army or to the entry into a military alliance. #ADNcat

41. Defense in stateless nations. The Catalan case

If Catalonia reaches its independence with the nonviolent force of the people (is here another way?) it must be defended with this same force. But this nonviolent force can only be if, from now on, it is organized for these two objectives. As we will see, the proposal to create territorial groupings of Nonviolent Self-Defense is a step towards the first objective that, with independence, will be the basis of a Catalan Nonviolent Civil Defense. #ADNcat

42. Now, in the Catalan case, who do we have to defend ourselves against?

If we consider Catalonia as an occupied country, we have to defend ourselves from: 1. the Spanish State that maintains the political occupation with an unalterable legal framework and with the financial, judicial and repressive systems at its disposal. 2. The transnationals - including the Spanish and Catalan ones - that maintain the economic and cultural occupation with the control of investments, the threat to the workplaces and the Hispanic-globalizing acculturation. 3. The lack of social and national cohesion, the imbalances of all kinds, which increase

the conflicts between sectors of the population of different or-
igins, languages, classes... attacked by the forces of the Spanish
State that want to maintain the country's unity. Not only "one
is Catalan who lives and works in Catalonia", but Catalan is also
who, at least, respects Catalonia; and, to respect a country, one
has to be treated with dignity. #ADNcat

43. In a Catalan republic, from whom would we have to defend ourselves?

In the case of a Catalan Republic, the only threat to territorial
integrity would be the reaction of the Spanish State itself and its
Armed Forces. No other neighboring country would be a threat
to be taken into account, except if we were to open to NATO's
enemies, in case the Catalan Republic were to be part of it.

To face the threat of the Spanish Armed Forces, an independent
Catalonia (or in the process of being recognized) would have
no possibility of successfully confronting them, since it would
not have its own armed force and, in any case, it would be

impossible to create an effective defensive capability, without sufficient time having passed.

Therefore, the only realistic way to defend oneself from a military threat during the independence process, or after independence, is to have created a nonviolent citizen force, well organized, to apply the dissuasive and resistance possibilities of the Civilian Way of Nonviolent Defense; a possible creation now, within a legal framework, that would not be as easy to prevent as if it were, obviously, the creation of an armed force.

Laying the foundations of a Civilian Way of Nonviolent Defense, promoting, as we will see, Nonviolent Self-Defense groups, requires little money and has fewer risks than other ways, being a self-defense without weapons, or any use of violence. Focused on the defense of aggressions against human, political, social and environmental rights, it is, at the same time, a tool to strengthen social cohesion, a basic condition for the success of any Nonviolent Defense. #ADNcat

44. In a Catalan republic, how to contribute to human security and peace?

The contribution to European common security must be part of global human security and, therefore, in the name of the former we cannot participate in policies or operations that jeopardize global security, as some European states tend to do, with or without NATO. A demilitarized, neutral country with a nonviolent civil defense in Europe could be the best contribution to peace and global security.

Whether this neutrality would hinder the recognition of the Catalan Republic as a new state in Europe will depend on the role that the nonviolent force of the people will have had in achieving independence. If it has been decisive (what else, otherwise?) it will have gained respect and confidence in being a force for dissuasion, and even more, it could be a model exportable to other places and processes. #ADNcat

Part 3

WHAT WE CAN DO NOW AND HERE: NONVIOLENT SELF-DEFENSE (ADN)

45. What is Nonviolent Self-Defense (ADN)?

The organization of Nonviolent Self-Defense is an implementation of the civilian way of civil defense. Unlike the Ministries of Defense (of War?) with policies that are not only defensive, but also violently offensive - because of the type of weapons and operations they carry out -, Nonviolent Self-Defense can only be defensive, it is only to protect people, their rights, institutions and the territory where they live, from any aggression. #ADNcat

46. What inspires Nonviolent Self-Defense (ADN)?

Nonviolent Self-Defense aims to lay the foundations of a Civil Nonviolent Defense System inspired by historical experiences, such as those mentioned above, and by the different proposals elaborated by Gonzalo Arias (The Anti-Coup and Tomorrow's Bloodless Army) and Gene Sharp (Nonviolent Civilian-based defense) as well as studies done in Catalonia, such as A safe state and in peace *(Un estat segur i en pau)*, all of them published in large part by the Institut Català Internacional per la Pau. #ADNcat

ADN is a proposal of citizen organization inspired by initiatives such as the Tree of Assemblies (Xirinacs), We are people and we decide, Sociocràcia, Convivialisme, the Manifest Re-evolució noviolenta o extermini or Communal Democracy. ADN is committed to balancing human relationships with the nature of which we are part, and therefore renounces undertaking all kinds of aggressions and violence to achieve its objectives. #ADNcat

Civilian Nonviolent Defense System

https://lluitanoviolenta.cat/projecte-defensa-noviolenta

A Civilian System of Nonviolent Defense as an alternative to Military Systems of Violent Defense

It cannot be that, in the face of yet another war, for lack of a Civil Nonviolent Defense alternative, the population can only choose

47. What is the indicator of balanced relationships?

A key indicator to know the degree of balanced relationships in a territory (street, neighborhood, village, town, city, region, nation, continent, world...) is the degree of social and natural cohesion of the people who live there. A strong community cohesion is the result of a high level of covered human needs that makes this territory a strong habitable space for everyone, and therefore, a space worth defending. #ADNcat

---

between supporting the war (with more weapons, more soldiers, more budget...) or clamoring to stop the war (with more anti-militarist and disarmament demonstrations, more calls for dialogue, more analysis on the causes of war...).

In the last 100 years there have been many experiences, studies and proposals around the world to lay the foundations of a **Civilian Nonviolent Defense System** as an alternative to the usual Military Systems of Violent Defense.

The alternative is possible. This project, if it obtains the necessary contribution and citizen's involvement, wants to propose what this Civil Nonviolent Defense System could be like in Catalonia, both in the current phase and in the case of the emergence of an independent state.

A dozen of books are recommended, the background is exposed and it is proposed how to start a ADN.

Gonzalo Arias Bonet

https://lluitanoviolenta.cat/
autor/arias-bonet-gonzalo

Gonzalo Arias was one of the pioneers of nonviolence in Spain and writer of a dozen books from his nonviolent and Christian vision.

He was born into a middle-class family. He finished his law degree, but when he was more interested in a diplomatic career, he moved to Paris where he worked as a translator for the Ministry of Information and UNESCO.

In Paris he discovered the book *L'Action Nonviolente* by Joseph Pyronnet, which changed his Christian vision and the discovery of nonviolence that marked him forever. His first book *Los encartelados, a program novel* (March 1968 in France) was distributed clandestinely. Gonzalo Arias himself made the fictional character come true on October 20, 1968 in Madrid. As a result, he was arrested and sentenced to seven months in prison and a fine of twelve thousand pesetas. This was the first explicitly nonviolent action to be carried out in Spain.

In 1971 he participated in a march to support conscientious objectors to military service and in 1976 he publicly denounced police torture. He wrote several books to provide a theoretical basis for the nonviolent movement.

The anti-coup. Manual for nonviolent resistance to a coup d'état

https://lluitanoviolenta.cat/recurs/el-antigolpe-manual-para-la-respuesta-noviolenta-un-golpe-de-estado

What would a population have to do to defend itself from the military and political collusion? *El antigolpe* was one of the few books that tried to answer this question after the attempted coup d'état of February 23rd 1981 in the middle of the Spanish democratic transition. Hence the importance of this work that Gonzalo Arias had to edit on his own after twelve publishers refused to publish it.

The book raises questions that are still relevant today: the hierarchical nature and the lines of obedience to the armed forces, the study of failed attempts of coup d'état through the practice of disobedience inside and outside the army, and the examination of past crimes in order to analyze what went wrong in the popular resistance.

Tomorrow's bloodless army

https://lluitanoviolenta.cat/recurs/
el-ejercito-incruento-de-manana-
materiales-para-un-debate-sobre-
un-nuevo-modelo-de-defensa-1

Gonzalo Arias collects different proposals on civil defense and suggests how a defensive organization could be armed with volunteers trained in the strategies and tactics of nonviolent struggle.

Nonviolent Civilian-based defense

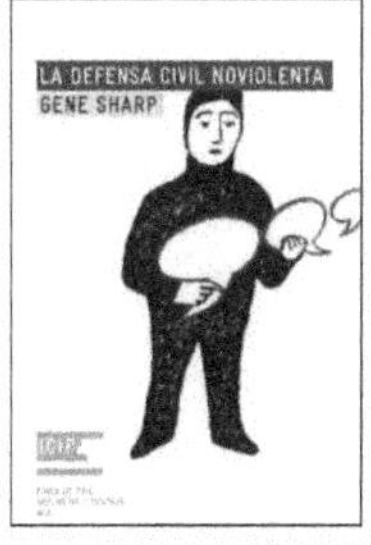

https://www.nonviolent-conflict.org/
resource/civilian-based-defense-a-
post-military-weapons-system/

The Baltic countries, Lithuania, Latvia and Estonia, declared their independence in 1990 and faced an attempt of aggression from the Soviet authorities. During the crisis, the three governments relied heavily on the methods of nonviolent resistance they had learned from the writings of Gene Sharp. In that situation, Andreus Butkevicius, the Lithuanian Minister of Defense, quoting Gene Sharp's book, proclaimed: "I would rather have this book than an atomic bomb".

The nonviolent Civilian-based defense compiles and reviews the most significant conflicts faced with nonviolent means until 1990. It also exposes the keys that would allow the foundation of a nonviolent civilian response to two types of conflicts: coups d'état and invasions. After almost three decades, many events have corroborated Gene Sharp's proposals in a multitude of conflicts, showing that a nonviolent response to face both threats is possible and that it is in the hands of any people, especially if they are prepared.

Tree of the assemblies

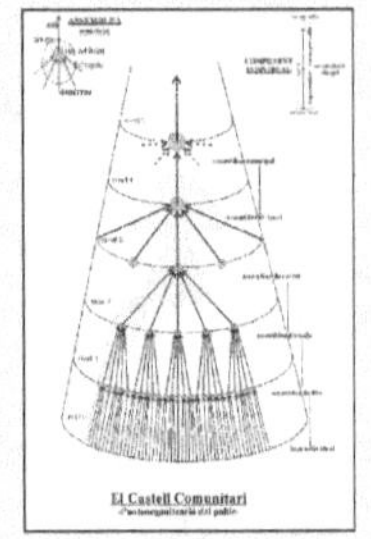

http://chalaux.org/demotica/
xdemctin.htm

Documents that are part of the strategy of achievement elaborated by Lluís Maria Xirinacs, based on a Tree of Assemblies, to vertebrate the people of each nation and fight for their liberation, practicing nonviolence.

We are people and we decide

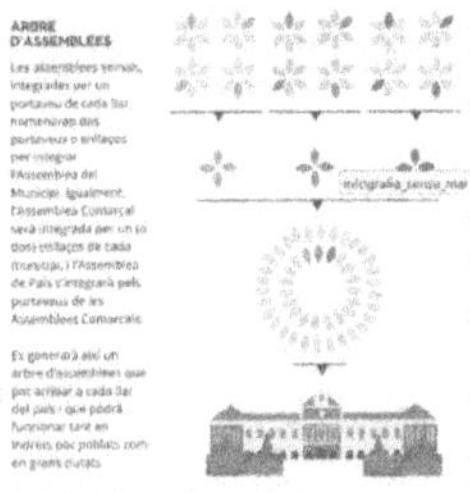

https://www.sompobleidecidim.cat/

An initiative that tries to put into practice the Tree of Assemblies in the current context: Here and now, we are the voice and the strength of the people: participate in the constituent dialogues throughout the country on climate, housing, gender equality, economy and participatory democracy. Let's exercise the people's democracy and make it binding in the final multi-referendum.

48. What are the objectives of an ADN to strengthen community cohesion?

The ADN of each territory - from the street to the city... - con-tributes, directly or through political pressure, to every person who lives there, at least:

1. Not going hungry or thirsty, is not malnourished and eat healthily.
2. Not suffering extreme cold or heat, have adequate clothing and a decent roof.
3. Not being neglected or discriminated against for any personal or group diversity or origin.
4. Having a free, dignified and useful occupation, with an income adequate to their needs and possibilities.
5. Having adequate care and treatment to cope with any illness.
6. Having access to true knowledge and information appropriate to their interests.
7. Freely and responsibly expressing their opinions and prefer-ences.
8. Being able to influence and participate in community and po-litical decisions in different areas.
9. Not being assaulted or suffering violence with impunity with-out protection, and being able to be rescued.
10. Living in a non-degraded environment where we do not harm the air, water, soil, flora and fauna.

#ADNcat

Building a safe and peaceful state of the world

https://lluitanoviolenta.cat/recurs/
construir-un-estat-segur-i-en-pau

Building a secure and peaceful state is a contribution to the social dialogue on the security and defense of states. It aims to provide arguments so that both existing states and newly created ones, as may be the case of Catalonia in the future, address conflicts from a non-military perspective and abandon armed defense as a pillar of human security.

For three years a group of people in the field of peace from different organizations and collectives in Catalonia shared reflections and ideas in order to find common formulations for the concepts discussed. The Seminari Estat de Pau, heir of the Pau i Treva collective, was created in September 2012 to respond to the concerns of Catalan social movements in the face of a pro-sovereignty process that wanted to be radical in its approach but profoundly peaceful, democratic and nonviolent in its forms.

49. What does ADN count on to advance in these objectives?

ADN uses the capabilities of the **nonviolent way**:

- **Awareness** of interconnectedness, and respect, between all people and living things
- **Empathic communication** in interpersonal relationships and social conflicts.
- **Nonviolent struggle** to confront the violation of rights and freedoms
- **Nonviolent civil resistance** to confront violent aggressions
- **Nonviolent civil defense** to confront invasions and armed occupations

  #ADNcat

50. What are the key elements of nonviolent struggle? (LNV)

The **LNV** (Nonviolent struggle in Catalan acronym) has to have an equitable and true objective, but it needs:

- **Strategy:** how we will achieve the objective we want to reach
- **Attitude:** how we arouse empathy and get many people to support the cause.
- **Campaigns:** how to articulate different actions into clear messages
- **Actions:** how to focus energy on achievable objectives that will lead us to the general one
- **Techniques:** how we train and exercise skills to carry out actions successfully.

  #ADNcat

Global nonviolent re-evolution or total extermination

A new and great global re-evolution is emerging and it is imperative to ensure the almost inexorable total self-extermination of the current civilization and of a great part of the life forms, especially the human one, on planet Earth.

https://lluitanoviolenta.cat/re-evolucio-noviolenta-o-extermini

A re-evolution, understood as a set of rapid, drastic, effective, individual and collective evolutions that affect the globality of human inter-relationships and of these with nature.

A post-violent re-evolution, which does not count on violence because it considers it a recessive character of humanization, a patriarchal and male chauvinism characteristic to overcome.

Institut Català Internacional per la Pau

https://www.icip.cat/ca/?s=noviolencia

The Institut Català Internacional per la Pau is a public and independent institution, created by the Parliament of Catalonia in 2007, with the aim of promoting the culture of peace in Catalan society and internationally, and to ensure that Catalonia plays an active role as an agent of peace in the world.

The ICIP is an autonomous organization with its own legal personality. It provides services to public administrations, academia and civil society, and reports to Parliament, the Government and the general public.

Among the numerous publications, books and studies on nonviolence stand out.

Communal Democracy

https://directa.cat/una-forca-collectiva-per-a-tres-combats/

The new institutions of communal democracy, as a result of the confluence of the local political, social, economic and cultural fabric, will have to exercise collective self-determination in all areas of life, as a practical exercise of resolution of the social, economic, cultural and ecological needs of the population, and they will have to do it from a delicate balance: maintaining their own autonomy, avoiding the servitudes of institutional politics, without underestimating a necessary intervention in the existing political institutions. That is, without renouncing to submitting them to a deep democratization, and without renouncing to sustain, materially and discursively, scenarios of general self-determination, key in the configuration of the social majorities of our country.

51. What types of actions or campaigns does nonviolent struggle combine?

- **Dialogue:** always talk to the adversary, before, during and after...
- **Denunciation:** need to bring awareness about the conflict, to show the imbalances...
- **Non-cooperation:** withdrawal of collaboration towards the adversary, without doing anything illegal...
- **Civil disobedience:** stop submitting to unjust laws or norms, by assuming the risks
- **Creation of alternatives:** show what life would be like if the denounced injustice were over.

#ADNcat

52. How is ADN organized in each place?

ADN is self-organized in small, voluntary, volunteer **groups** of people who work together:

- **Diagnosis** of the imbalances with a **'triage'** of those that are most serious, which, at the same time, can be solved.
- **Resilience plan** to reduce imbalances and aggressions, starting with the most viable ones.
- **Formation,** training and organization in the nonviolent way
- Nonviolent defense and territorial balance **campaigns** to implement the plan.
- **Coordination** with other ADNs to broaden the impact of the campaigns.

#ADNcat

53. What are the objectives and relationships of a ADN?

Each ADN strives for balanced relationships among its members and ensures their participation both in the orientation of priorities and in the effectiveness of actions. It fosters mutual esteem and empathy: only defending what each feels part of. Each ADN aspires to extend this closeness to the whole country and the whole world; it understands its actions as contributions to the balances that make the Earth a habitable planet for everyone. #ADNcat

54. What does it mean to commit to a ADN?

The members of an ADN are committed to sign and make effective the Declaration of Commitment and to welcome all the people who wish to assume it and to get involved in it. They are organized sociocracy: the "associated" people seek to complement the participatory involvement both in the deliberative making of decisions, and in the operative execution of them. #ADNcat

55. What does it mean to say that ADNs function and are coordinated sociocratically?

The ADNs are formed in loops of up to 7 members, they make decisions by consent (no one against), including the trio of responsible persons - secretary, coordination and 2 liaisons - without prior nominations. The link from each circle to the most internal circles provides the vision of the most external circles, the link from the internal circles to the external circles, provides the operative coordination of the decisions made. #ADNcat

56. Experience and relevance in previous struggles is a good basis for ADN

Organizing the ADN is not improvised, it is necessary to count on people, organizations and decentralized networks that have experience in nonviolent struggles in defense of territory, housing, labor, environmental, climate, cultural, linguistic conflicts.... for human, social, national, women's, migrants' rights; against armament, debt, consumerism and the great planetary imbalances.

The people who fight every day for social cohesion, for respect for the natural environment, for the eco-social transition are the basis of the Nonviolent Self-Defense, because these struggles are the best school of active and responsible citizenship, essential for the defense of the country. But ADNs are open to anyone who wants to get involved, whether they have experience or not, because they will be the common learning space. #ADNcat

Sociocracy

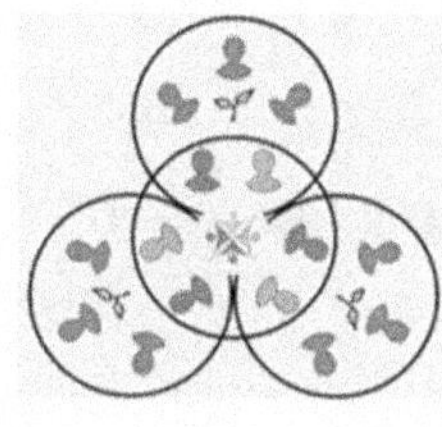 

https://lluitanoviolenta.cat/recurs/
las-fuerzas-creativas-de-la-auto-
organizacion-y-sociocracia-para-
organizaciones-sin-animo-de

https://en.wikipedia.org/wiki/
Sociocracy

The grassroots groups choose, without candidates, their link to the most central group to provide legitimacy and the central group chooses its link to the grassroots groups to provide effectiveness.

Demo-cracy (common people, as the primary source of political power); Socio-cracy (associates as ruling class). To complement effectiveness (vertical) with legitimacy (horizontal).

4 elements: circles, double link (↑↓), no nominations, by consent. If group cohesion is very important, better to agree on decisions without objections - fundamental oppositions.

Part 4

MORE ABOUT OBJECTIVES AND TECHNIQUES OF NONVIOLENT CIVIL DEFENSE

We resume ideas very well expressed by Maciej Bartkowski, in the above-mentioned article of 2015

57. Objectives of nonviolent civil defense

To counter an invasion: 1. To prevent or delay the adversary from achieving its immediate objectives. 2. To undermine the ability of the adversary to continue its invasion. 3. To build unity, civic solidarity and discipline, while organizing the nonviolent resistance of the citizenry in case of externally provoked disturbances or in case of invasion and occupation; 4. To protect democratic practices while the struggle lasts. #ADNcat

58. What are the territorial defense techniques in case of invasion?

From historical examples we can learn different techniques that make sense in a clear and public strategy of nonviolent civil defense. We have an extensive collection of interesting and evocative examples of all kinds of nonviolent struggles and tactics. Below we will highlight some specific ones on how to confront invasions. #ADNcat

Civil Resistance Practices in the 21st Century

https://www.nonviolent-conflict.
org/webinar-civil-resistance-
tactics-in-the-21st-century/

The ever-expanding repertoire of nonviolent tactics is a testament to the genius and creativity of activists around the world. The exploration of new tactics - the main purpose of this monograph - is not simply an exercise in documentation or classification. The study of each individual method opens the door to a world of stories about civil resistance in different places and times. Each method offers a glimpse into the perseverance and resilience of people in the face of repression, which demonstrates not only a drive to fight for rights, freedom and justice, but also the need for innovation and adaptation in leading resistance struggles.

59. Human walls and blocking of communication routes

Preparing and training citizens to: 1. The rapid deployment of unarmed people to build "human walls" to defend public administrations and communication centers. 2. The blockade of railroads, roads, ports or airports to stop the adversary's attacks. 3. The mobilization of thousands of automobiles to obstruct the transport and circulation of the adversary and to be able to reach the people with information and help. #ADNcat

60. Not cooperating with the authorities usurped by the occupant

Encouraging non-cooperation towards the usurpers with less risky actions such as those practiced by the Danes and Czechoslovakians: stike of "Sit-down strikes", absence in social and political events important to the adversary, carrying national symbols, isolating the occupation forces, mass resignations in the usurped administrations, refusal to understand instructions from the usurped government and to implement them effectively. #ADNcat

61. The costs of non-cooperation make the invasion unprofitable

When the occupier encounters non-cooperation in key sectors of society and the economy, he has to face enormous costs to replace with his own personnel the work that the non-cooperation is not doing, causing it to cease to be economically profitable. In 1923 in the Ruhr, the refusal of the German railways to transport coal to France and Belgium forced the mobilization of more than 10,000 civil servants from these two states. #ADNcat

Global database of nonviolent action

https://lluitanoviolenta.cat/recurs/
global-nonviolent-action-database-3

It offers free access to information on hundreds of cases of nonviolent action, from all continents and most countries, for learning and citizen action. The database is a Swarthmore College project.

62. To provoke the moral weakening of the bases of the adversary

Or generate disaffection, internal dissidence and mass desertions among the adversary's troops and allies, including business, religious and cultural organizations, as well as their families. Or, actions to build trust, increase fraternity between locals and troops of the adversary, counter the adversary's war propaganda and reduce the social distance between the population of both sides.

The ultimate goal is to increase unrest and, ultimately, an open opposition of the population to the actions of their government abroad. This is easier to achieve if the targeted population maintains nonviolent discipline. This strategy makes it much more difficult for the opponent to rationalize their vilification of the attacked population and to achieve their own internal support for the aggression abroad. #ADNcat

63. Governments that bet on Nonviolent Civil Defense

A government that is committed to nonviolent civil defense can distribute a manual like the one in Lithuania, and organize routine training exercises in which the civilian population practices these measures. It can also support the creation of a civilian resistance infrastructure that would allow it to strengthen defensive capabilities and thus contribute to the credibility of a strategy of dissuasion through radical non-cooperation. #ADNcat

64. Avoid the simultaneous application of the two defenses, nonviolent and violent

The government that supports civil defense must avoid the simultaneous use of both forms of resistance, nonviolent and violent: if necessary, it could apply them at different moments of the conflict or apply them in different places. For example, civil defense would be organized in the cities, while the army would be limited to certain rural areas, in order to reduce civilian casualties and the destruction of cities. #ADNcat

65. Nonviolent civil defense strengthens democracy after the invasion is over

It promotes national and local democracy and democratic practices. In fact, nonviolent civil defense can produce significant democratic dividends for countries that adopt it. Recent studies have shown that the practice of nonviolent resistance will increase the chances of a democratic outcome in these countries five years after the end of the conflict by a factor of two. #ADNcat

Why Civil Resistance Works

https://cup.columbia.edu/
book/why-civil-resistance-
works/9780231156820

Why Civil Resistance Works: the Strategic Logic of NonViolent Conflict, Erica Chenoweth and Maria J. Stephan, study this impact, secondary, but no less important to consolidate the post armed conflict.

66. On which actors is the nonviolent civil defense based

Effective civil defense is based on self-organized and decentralized civil defense networks. In this sense, any support to the development of national civil defense strategies will at the same time reinforce coalition building, civic engagement and the associative life of local and regional communities, including a greater strength of civil society institutions. #ADNcat

67. Communication and information are also decisive in this defense.

Communication and information are very important to this advocacy effort. Authorities at all levels of government must work with civil society to ensure that information continues to flow to and from them. National and local public administrations must play a crucial role in supporting and implementing specific guidelines for nonviolent action in the event of an invasion.

As armies say, that "every soldier is a sensor," each person must gather information about enemy troop movements, repressive actions and atrocities they commit, as well as nonviolent actions in preparation or underway. A number of local media centers can gather, verify and relay this information to citizens in other parts of the country and beyond. #ADNcat

68. Nonviolent civil defense can't avoid having victims

Nonviolent actions can have victims. The killing of unarmed civilians in disciplined actions of civil resistance can create moral and political outrage, not only among the troops of the adversary, but also among its public and the international community. It can clearly demonstrate which side is violent and which side is unarmed defense, reducing the fog of war and the effectiveness of the adversary's propaganda. #ADNcat

Part 5

A GOVERNMENTAL NONVIOLENT CIVIL DEFENSE

It gathers key ideas of the unpublished proposal elaborated by Santi Martí, member of NOVACT's Board and member of the Col·lectiu Pau i Treva (collective for Peace and Truce).

69. Nonviolent civilian self-defense can improve defense policies

As we have seen, nonviolent civil defense has been theorized and its elements have been practiced throughout numerous conflicts during the last century. Democratic states and their societies should not ignore this set of knowledge and practices to improve their defense and security. If they ignore them they will be under suspicion of being dominated by the corrupting political-media-military-industrial complex. #ADNcat

70. How to organize a Nonviolent Civil Defense from the government?

In case a government considers that without a Civilian Nonviolent Defense it will not be able to achieve or maintain the sovereignty to which the people aspire, there are proposals that can facilitate its implementation as one of the main structures of the state. We will highlight elements to be taken into account on objectives and organic structure of a defense exclusively by civilian nonviolent actions, complementary to the internal security system #ADNcat.

71. An unprecedented option but a necessary alternative?

We have no references of any state that has a defense system based exclusively on nonviolent civilian actions with the real objective of facing hypothetical aggressions or invasions with a permanent and stable institutional and administrative structure and, obviously, financed from public budgets. But the failure of conventional defense systems urges us to consider it.

It is worth noting that the theory elaborated on civilian action defense models and, above all, their practical implementation is very limited. Designing a complete civilian action defense system for a state, we can qualify it, at least, as unprecedented; it implies a paradigm shift in the defense policies so far applied from the states. Many of the necessary concretions can only be made by passing through it. #ADNcat

72. When a military defense is not available, it is better to build a civilian one?

The known experiences have never been substitutes of the military option, they have been complementary to the usual military system. As we have seen, there have only been some partial experiences that over time have been diluted within the military defense system and have remained fundamentally dedicated to civil protection and emergency tasks. #ADNcat

73. Civil Defense is complementary to the human security system.

Despite the connections with defense, we will not go into the design of the other broad areas of protection of human security: ensuring internal coexistence (police), the control of territorial limits; environmental protection and custody of the natural environment and territory; emergencies, rescue and civil protection; food and energy security; intercultural cooperation and solidarity. #ADNcat

74. A system of Nonviolent Civil Defense for Catalonia, key state structure

We will make an approach on the construction of a governmental initiative for a defense system by nonviolent actions, in the context of the construction of the state structures for an independent Catalonia. We will not go into justifying or discussing the relevance or not of providing the future Catalan state with a defense system of this type. We only provide feasibility ideas to help make the decision. #ADNcat

75. Official and real objectives of any defense system

Any national defense system has the same "official" objectives: to protect and secure the lives of the population, to preserve the continuity of its administrative structures and to maintain effective control over its territory. To achieve them it is necessary to establish the objectives of the defense policy: the first is to have a deterrence system that avoids a possible aggression, occupation or invasion.

But the European political-military-industrial apparatus has under the defense policy, at least 5 functions: 1. The official one, dissuasion, (now again, in front of the Russian threat). 2. The economic-political one of the armament business and power. 3. The creation of a European superpower (allied with NATO?). 4. That of preserving the privileges of exploitation of the countries of the global South. 5. Stabilization of authority in domestic politics. #ADNcat

76. Conditions to make effective the dissuasion with the Nonviolent Civil Defense

In a system of defense by civil actions there are two essential conditions to make effective and credible the dissuasion: the cohesion of the social and territorial environment to be defended and the ethics of the relationship with the rest of the world. Cohesion is achieved by creating the conditions of relevance and therefore of national identification; the ethics is that the country seeks balanced global relations.

These conditions require a deepening of the democratic values and principles of universal justice, equality before the law and equality of opportunity, as well as solidarity among the members of the community. In this sense, education, the social welfare system and the social communication system play a central role.

The ethics of the relationship between the country and the world must be clearly contained in the constitution of the state: the renunciation of war, threats and the use of armed force in the resolution of international conflicts but, at the same time, the active contribution in the construction of peace in the world, also in other areas, such as the economic and the rights of foreigners, which must be ethically irreproachable.

As dissuasion can become insufficient, the defense system must be aware, in the most effective way possible, of what it means to defend itself: identify and evaluate the potential dangers and threats, prevent them, protect itself, try to suppress them and, if necessary, neutralize the attacks, hinder the invasion, make the occupation unfeasible and put an end to them. #ADNcat

77. On the incompatibility of strategies and actions that are both violent and nonviolent

It is necessary to separate nonviolent actions from any violent action, which will be labeled as "terrorist". Otherwise, as experience shows, any violent action can delegitimize the nonviolent resistance of the whole and produce repression on both. It is necessary to elucidate the position to take in each case in front of the actions of sabotage with "violence" on things, which obviously affect people. #ADNcat

78. On the knowledge of nonviolent defense strategies

As we have seen, there is already an important analysis of historical nonviolent practices and applied nonviolent strategies that have formed a solid theoretical framework. However, it is important to note the need to delve much deeper into the theory, especially to specify how to apply them without improvisation and in a systematic way from state institutions and citizen organizations, in a changing society and world. #ADNcat

79. On favorable and unfavorable stakeholders

We already know that a defense system based on a nonviolent policy must count on the participation of the entire social fabric: public institutions, civil organizations and the entire citizenry. Inevitably, it is necessary to take into consideration the existence of indifferent, neutral, adversaries and "collaborators". It is necessary to know how to confront them without unleashing or justifying arbitrary internal repressions based on rumors and vendettas. #ADNcat

80. On the tools to be used and the infrastructure of civil defense

Although the policy of nonviolent defense is based on civilian actions as the main weapons to face aggressions, it must have technical means and infrastructures for protection or bloodless defense such as all kinds of shields, hiding places, shelters, surveillance and alarm systems, communication and counter-information systems, data processing, alternative transportation... #ADNcat

81. On economic sovereignty

And, therefore, together with the adoption of defense by civil actions, it seems necessary to build a knowledge, industrial and service sector wise, to ensure technological development and the capacity for autonomous supply. And, above all, to have built a sovereign economy in all the key and strategic sectors (food, energy, communications, finances...) that avoid dependencies and are weak points for its defense and human security. #ADNcat

82. Organization and structure: command, policy and operations

The defense command must have a hierarchical structure in order to be as effective and efficient as possible. Nevertheless, it must be based on decentralization and territorial and sectorial autonomy, both in the definition of policy and in the implementation of actions. It is necessary to define the competency limits and apply the dynamics of sociocracy that allow complementing the operational effectiveness and participatory legitimacy.

It is necessary to differentiate between two organizational spheres: the political and the operational. The former analyzes, designs and decides defense policies and the strategic direction of defense and foreign action for peace, the latter executes them. The first arises from the democratic will of the citizens and is under parliamentary control. Territorially the administrations of the communities, counties and municipalities must be incardinated.

The second is mixed, a part of the administration, staffed by technicians and civil servants, and the other part is a group of volunteers for Nonviolent Self-Defense with a territorial and sectorial structure. The command of the first corresponds to the President of Catalonia assisted by a Minister of Peace and Defense. The command of the second corresponds to the Chief of the Peace Forces, appointed by the government with dependence from a Minister.

The budget will include resources for both structures. It will be necessary to evaluate the needs in human and economic resources, but they will be much lower than those required for a military defense system. The Ministry will have units specialized in, among others: studies, plans and strategies, education and training, intelligence, cooperation for peace, communication and data systems, logistics, infrastructure and engineering. #ADNcat

83. Collegiate participation bodies for sectorial and territorial coordination

In the absence of conflict, the bodies may have the following functions: monitoring and warning of dangers, risks and threats; analysis of their contribution to civil defense; participation in the elaboration of contingency plans in their area of competence; and remaining ready to act in the action operations entrusted to them. These plans will establish the lines of command and functions of its members.

In case of conflict, they will carry out the actions foreseen in the respective contingency plans with the degree of autonomy and coordination contemplated. At the sectorial level, the involvement of: universities and centers of knowledge, associations and NGOs, companies, workers, peasants, media, educational centers, health centers, police and civil protection...

The different territorial administrative units –municipality and neighborhood (depending on the size), county, district...– will have a Nonviolent Self-Defense corps that will integrate the volunteers that will be assigned to it under the operational command of its head and in sociocratic coordination with the corps of the other territorial units. #ADNcat

Part 6

INSPIRING EXPERIENCES OF CITIZEN DEFENSE

84. What precedents do we know of nonviolent armies?

In the last 100 years we highlight three: 1. **Shanti Sena** "peace army" raised by Gandhi in India (their nonviolent methods have been adopted, as we can see, by Peace Brigades International, Nonviolent Peaceforce, Swaraj Peeth); 2. **Khudai Khidmatgar** (literally Servants of God), also known as "Red Shirts" of the Muslim Pasthuns (ex Afghanistan) and, 3. **Guardia indígena del Cauca of Colombia** (Indigenous Guard of Cauca) since the last 23 years. #ADNcat

85. Shanti Sena / India's Gandhian Peace Corps

The Shanti Sena (peace army) is what Gandhi called the nonviolent peacekeeping volunteers (1922), during the Hindu-Muslim riots. Although Gandhi called for the creation of a "peace army" for national defense in 1942 –a plan that was never attempted, since the Japanese did not invade India–, the idea of Shanti Sena was linked to the struggle to minimize communal violence among the population.

In 1947, with independence, Gandhi proposed to organize a national Shanti Sena as a response to the riots that caused the death of half a million people when 10 million were expelled from their homes with the partition of India with Pakistan. Gandhi had invited hundreds of colleagues to organize the Shanti Sena in February 1948, but at the end of January, Gandhi was assassinated. The meeting was not held.

Vinoba, Gandhi's spiritual successor, founded Shanti Sena in 1957 to confront the disturbances that jeopardized Gandhian development. From 1962 to 1978 Narayan Desai was the director of Shanti Sena, which reached a maximum of 6,000 members in the mid-1960s; they were regular Gandhian development workers in rural areas, who could participate in actions when disturbances broke out in nearby villages. #ADNcat

86. Gandhian rules for satyagrahis to follow in a resistance campaign

Some of these rules are: live without anger; bear the wrath of your opponent; do not retaliate for attacks or chastisements; voluntarily submit yourself to arrest or confiscation of property; do not speak ill, or swear; do not insult your opponents; do not salute or insult your opponent's flag; if someone tries to insult or assault your opponent, defend him (by undertaking nonviolence) with your life.

As a prisoner, behave in a correct manner and obey prison regulations (except for those that are contrary to respect for oneself); do not demand special favor treatment; do not go on hunger strike in an attempt to improve conditions (that do not imply any harm to your dignity) of imprisonment. Obey with joy the civil disobedience orders of the leaders of the resistance campaign;

Do not choose which orders to obey, if you find that the action is immoral, do not do it at all; do not make your participation condition your companions, if you are in the campaign or in prison, do not expect support; don't be a cause of dispute, don't take part in it, help to show who is right; in interreligious conflict, give your life to protect (with nonviolence) those who are in danger on one side or the other; #ADNcat

87. Abdul Ghaffar Khan and the Red Shirts of the Pasthuns

Movement against the British Raj in colonial India led by Abdul Ghaffar Khan. He joined the All-India Muslim League and the National Congress of India. It played an important role in the Indian Independence Movement opposing the partition between India and Pakistan. It grew to 100,000 members. Initially, it was focused on social reform as a means to improve the status of the Pakistani people in British India.

He suffered many prohibitions and arrests. Khan recruited young men and women who had graduated from his schools. They were trained and uniformed volunteers who took an oath. They formed squads with officers and learned the basic discipline of an army, in this case nonviolent. The volunteers went to the villages and opened schools, helped in work projects and maintained order in the actions

Khan defended nonviolent protests and justified his actions in the Islamic context. He did not find Islam and nonviolence incompatible. The movement was inherently non-sectarian, with Muslims as well as some Hindu members. On more than one occasion when Hindus and Sikhs were attacked in Peshawar, Khan's red shirts helped protect their lives and property. #ADNcat

88. The oath of the Red Shirts of the Pasthuns

The oath of relevance includes: I promise to serve humanity in the name of God; to abstain from violence and revenge; to forgive those who oppress me or treat me cruelly; to abstain from participating in hatred and violence and to create enmity; to treat all people as brothers and friends; to abstain from antisocial customs and practices; to live a simple life, to practice virtue and to abstain from evil;

And the oath continued: to behave well and not lead an idle life; to dedicate at least two hours a day to social work; to sacrifice my wealth, life and comfort for the freedom of my nation and people; never to form part of factions, of hatred or jealousy of my people; I will stand by the side of the oppressed against the oppressor; I will not be a member of any other rival organization, nor will I form part of an armed army.

And it continued: I will faithfully obey all the legitimate orders of my officials; I will live according to the principles of nonviolence; I will serve all of God's creatures equally; my goal will be the attainment of the freedom of my country and my religion; I will always strive to do what is right and good; I will never desire any reward for my service; all my efforts will be to please God and not for any glory or victory. #ADNcat

89. Indigenous Guard of Cauca (Colombia)

The Indigenous Guard is a community protection network formed by women, men, boys and girls who defend their territories peacefully, protect their autonomy and ancestral lands. It is an unarmed security force that has been patrolling its territories since 1999, as one of the forms of resistance to violence. Set in motion by indigenous associations such as CRIC (Consejo Regional Indígena del Norte del Cauca).

It is at the service of the CRIC's objectives: to recover and expand the land of the "resguardos", to defend the ancestral territory and living spaces; to strengthen the indigenous "cabildos"; to make known the laws on indigenous people and demand their application; to defend history, language and customs; to train indigenous teachers; to strengthen community enterprises; to recover, defend and protect the living spaces in harmony and balance with Mother Earth.

The Indigenous Guard carries out surveillance work to detect the presence of guerrillas, paramilitaries, drug traffickers or the army in their territories; it has a communication network to raise the alarm if there are indications of armed groups; it patrols in small motorcycle groups. Normally the volunteers that make up this security force have received training and have participated in community rituals. It is made up of thousands of people.

The Indigenous Guard can also confront armed groups and the army, usually using intimidation tactics due to numerical

https://www.cric-colombia.org/
portal/estructura-organizativa/
plataforma-de-lucha/

https://www.ccma.
cat/tv3/alacarta/30-
minuts/morir-pels-
drets/video/6190763/

superiority, and has even expelled them several times from their territory; it has also released people under arrest and children forced to join armed groups; and dismantled clandestine cocaine laboratories. Watch recent 30' TV documentary.

The Indigenous Guard is characterized by not carrying weapons and wears as a symbol of identity a handkerchief with the colors of the indigenous organization (green and red in the case of the CRIC) and a baton. This is a stick with colored belts that can also be used to create containment barriers in demonstrations where violent confrontation is expected by the police with each "guard" holding his company's baton. #ADNcat

90. Different attempts to approach nonviolent civilian defense

We have already seen several initiatives and experiences that in the 20th century have shown the need and the possibility of a nonviolent civil defense. Inspired by them, several authors have researched, written and formulated proposals in different countries. Among them, Gonzalo Arias. In 1977 he made a compilation in *Defensa armada o Defensa popular Noviolenta (Armed Defense or Nonviolent Popular Defense)*. Updated in El antigolpe (The anti-coup), 1982 and El ejército incruento de mañana (The bloodless army of tomorrow), 1995. #ADNcat

91. Different attempts to approach a nonviolent civil defense. Gonzalo Arias

Gonzalo Arias, especially in *El ejército incruento de mañana*, reviews the different theories and experiences. He puts forward his own proposal of a bloodless army, with 3 characteristics: voluntarism (anti-conscription), renunciation of lethal weapons (anti-weaponism, anti-ecological and destructive), and, nowadays we would say wasteful, feminism (anti-sexism).

A bloodless army of voluntary people, with a discipline based on responsibility, coming from: the pacifist and nonviolent movement; from disappointed military people who do not see their violent contribution to peace; or, from former militants of armed struggle who have seen the limits. A violent person, Gandhi said, can understand nonviolence better than a coward.

Nonviolent civil defense is the refusal of a whole population to collaborate with the occupying power. We need training in nonviolent struggle and evolution of mentalities: we do not abandon the weapons of defense; we change them with the nonviolent force of the people! The population learns to defend itself in a different way, with attitudes and actions that take the initiative. The nonviolent struggle brings imagination to power.

Nonviolent defense dissociates itself from the pacifism, that considers that armies and weapons are the causes of war and that eliminating them would be the sufficient condition for peace. It is not enough to say no to war, it is necessary to create security alternatives. There is no more disarmament, we must move towards nonviolent transarmement. #ADNcat

92. Transarmament and the bloodless army. Gonzalo Arias

"Transarmament" is not a simple rejection of lethal weapons, but a process of progressive adoption of the "weapons" (tools), organization and practices of nonviolent civil defense and, therefore, a parallel reduction of offensive weapons, towards defensive weapons, until their substitution. The substitution of

lethal weapons by other weapons, immaterial but also material:
a) communication, b) civic disobedience and c) testimony.

a) Communication: the strength of the occupying government is based on disinformation and deception of its soldiers and population. It is necessary to be experts in counter-information, to know the occupying country and its language, its fallacious arguments, and to have the capacity to send clear and truthful messages about the meaninglessness of its invasive action through all possible channels.

b) Civic disobedience: a mature people knows how to say no to the invader's intentions. The members of the bloodless army must be clear about the conditions, limits and possibilities for its use, powerful and responsible, and train themselves to practice it: civic duty to disobey, strength of its massive application, difficulties when there is generalized fear, overcoming fear with gradual application, caution to avoid frivolizing the disobedience.

c) Testimony: the volunteers of this bloodless army must be willing to risk their lives, just as armed soldiers do. The difference is between the former bet on killing before being killed, and the latter that will speak and act without leaving any doubt that they will let themselves be killed before killing anyone. Being "martyr" (that means witness) is a powerful weapon to conquer the adversary and earn their respect. #ADNcat

93. The two disruptive ideas of nonviolent defense. Gonzalo Arias

It is based on unusual ideas: 1. it is not so much about defending the territory as defending the functioning of the institutions. Armed defense is based on the defense of the borders, if the enemy occupies the territory, all is lost. On the other hand, for nonviolent defense the territory is not so important, the real fight begins when the enemy has entered: it is necessary to avoid leaving the country's government in their hands. 2. The main weapon is organized disobedience. First it is necessary to counter-educate public servants and leaders, and the citizenry so that they have the courage to say "NO" to those who want to give orders with a gun in their hand. There may be deaths, nonviolent defense is not a child's play nor is it a guarantee of success –as neither is armed defense– but, in general, less blood will flow than in any armed resistance. #ADNcat

94. What nonviolent intervention forces do we know?

The "official" functions of the armies are not only to defend their own territory but also to intervene, in the best of cases, to maintain peace in conflicts in other countries. In this role, from the nonviolent perspective, we have already mentioned, inspired by Gandhi's Santi Sena, that several initiatives have been launched, such as: International Peace Brigades, Nonviolent Peaceforce and Civil Peace Services. #ADNcat

95. International Peace Brigades (PBI)

International Peace Brigades is an international organization founded in 1981. It provides protection to people facing attacks of various kinds because of their human rights activities, providing international accompaniment: physical presence with the threatened people, the creation of an international support network, dialogue with the authorities and the dissemination of information. So far, they have been to more than 12 countries. #ADNcat

https://www.pbi-ee.org/sobre-pbi-estado-espa%C3%B1ol

96. Nonviolent Peaceforce (NP)

Nonviolent Peaceforce, an organization founded in 2002, has the mission to protect civilians in violent conflict through unarmed strategies while helping local communities build Peace. NP is committed to a global culture of peace in which conflicts, within and between communities and countries, are managed through nonviolent means. It is guided by the principles of nonviolence, non-partisanship, primacy of local actors and civilian action. #ADNcat

https://nonviolentpeaceforce.org

97. Civil Peace Services (CPS)

Since the 1990s, proposals for the creation of Civil Peace Services (CPS) have emerged in various EU states with the support of public administrations; with the shared objective of improving the capacity of civil society to intervene and build opportunities for peace in violent international conflicts. In 2012 ICIP published a report on the feasibility of establishing a Catalan Civilian Nonviolent Peace Service. #ADNcat

A Nonviolent Civil Service

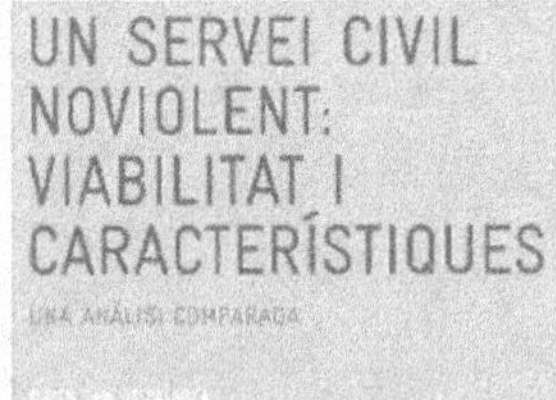

https://www.icip.cat/wp-content/uploads/2020/11/info2010_01_cat.pdf

98. A story to broaden perspectives: El planeta del foc (The Planet of Fire)

In this dramatic moment in which we have become aware that the thirty wars around the world, such as the one in Ukraine, cause atrocious and avoidable suffering in millions of people, we have rescued a story, The Planet of Fire, which invites young and old to reflect and act. If we, the inhabitants of the blue planet, do not organize ourselves to stop the wars, they will make us disappear as a species. It has versions and didactic guides. #ADNcat

Planet of Fire

https://lluitanoviolenta.cat/
el-planeta-del-foc

MANIFEST Catalunya per la seguretat humana i la pau (MANIFESTO Catalonia for human security and peace)

http://estatdepau.cat/pauitreva2/

http://estatdepau.cat/pauitreva2/video-roda-premsa-2/

Seminar on the State of Peace. Construir un estat segur i en pau

http://estatdepau.cat/pauitreva2/seminari-estat-de-pau-3/

https://www.icip.cat/ca/publication/construir-un-estat-segur-i-en-pau-seminari-estat-de-pau/

99. Col·lectiu Pau i Treva. Seminari Estat de Pau. (Peace and Truce Collective and Seminar State of Peace)

The vigil of the demonstration of September 11, 2012 called by the ANC, people of the Catalan movement for peace - Arcadi Oliveres, Pepe Beúnza, Alfons Banda... - reinforced the call for a peaceful and nonviolent attitude not only in the demonstration but also in the whole process towards sovereignty. From this fact arose the Pau i Treva collective that elaborated a manifesto presented on the 30th of January 2013 and that received more than 4000 supporters.

The Pau i Treva collective created the seminar Estat de Pau. The set of documents elaborated were collected in the book "Construir un estat segur i en pau. Com enfocar la seguretat i la defensa en un nou estat d'Europa" published in 2016 by the ICIP. It is the most complete work on the basis of Human Security and nonviolent civil defense applicable in Catalonia. #ADNcat

100. The Nonviolent Civil Defense project

It cannot be that in the face of war we can only choose between supporting the war (with more weapons, more soldiers, more budget) or wanting to stop the war (with demonstrations for disarmament, calls for dialogue, analysis of the causes of war). In the last 100 years there have been many experiences, studies and proposals around the world to lay the foundations of a Civilian Nonviolent Defense System as an alternative to Military Systems of Violent Defense. Let's go!

In the face of armed aggression, if we prepare ourselves, we can have better solutions than the spiral of war. There are those who say "If you don't want armed forces, you can't be independent and even less so with the neighbors that we have. Short and straight". And who answer: "If we achieved independence without an army, I don't see why we should have one to defend it". If you don't want a Nonviolent Self-Defense, you can't have independence or defend it. Short and straight. #ADNcat

AN INCREDIBLE STORY

As the subtitle of the **Nonviolent Self-Defense (ADN)** indicates, **in 100 short messages and an incredible story,** you will find enclosed this short story that opens the mind to another imaginary about how changes, human, social and political metamorphoses, take place.

An incredible story

Today has been the "D" day, or we could say, the "V" (V is for Verdad, - Truth in Spanish t.n.-) day, of Truth. What seemed impossible, has become reality. Many people in this small country have shown once again, as other times in history, that the super-power of humans works, well, it works when certain conditions are met.

These people a few years ago began to believe that:

1. Small changes, imperceptible as they are, accumulate and bring about great changes, metamorphoses. There is no pre-determined date, they evolve.

2. Human groups that share the same history, a story of an engrossing future, cooperate better to face any challenge, to build it.
3. Leaders are essential, but only if they are collective, only if everyone is essential, the movement does not feel when a leader falls or abandons it.
4. As in the great historical moments, each person feels part of a liberation army, but in this case, a nonviolent army, to generate new balances without provoking more imbalances or violence.

The "V" day has not been a date agreed in advance by anyone –like most of the previous "D" days–. It was the day on which the whole process of liberation, seen in many key areas of life, came to an end, like a flower blooming in spring. And, as in the life of a flower, this day is not the end of anything, but the beginning of the new process of turning from flower to fruit, and from fruit to flower, to start again...

In fact, we have lived many "V" days. Every time we have applied the four conditions, it has been a "V" day, a day of Truth.

Everything started in the darkest moment, when everything seemed lost. We were living in a state of emergency in many key areas of daily life, which was very difficult for many people, often for very different reasons. There were endemic imbalances that, for some people, meant having to go through hardship, being too cold or too hot, not having a home, living on the street, not having a decent job or income to survive, being excluded from health services, education, participation... while for other people these imbalances produced paradoxically opposite effects: malnutrition, obesity, circulatory or immune system disorders, work and life under permanent stress, insecurity in forgotten neighborhoods or in over-supervised mansions, over-information, therapeutic harassment, excess or lack of influence, excessiveness? Many people also adored the elites and success, even if it was to maintain at all costs their supposed wellbeing as an antidote to the danger of falling into the trap of the excluded. And some, others and those in the middle live under emergencies (which in many cases do not take into account social classes): the violence against women in a society that is still very patriarchal, the growing violence of the police, of the judicial and penitentiary system; of the armies and of the wars... and the perhaps not so perceptible violence of climate change, of the loss of biodiversity, of the 6th great extinction... but also caused by the concentration of power of the big digital and media platforms, of the banks and of the monetary/financial system, of the big transnational companies, of the aberrant investment funds...

The world war in Ukraine accelerated and aggregated all the imbalances that, without being fully aware of it, we had been experiencing: we confirmed what some had predicted, that our civilization was over-dependent on fossil fuels and suffered the climate change that we provoked with its waste, with the food industry, with mobility, with the temperature of "wellbeing" of our homes. The war will activate two opposite tendencies: it will increase the consumption of fossil fuels (such as coal, to try to survive the shortage and the increase of gas and oil prices) and at the same time it will activate the stagnant plans of renewable energies... All this will lead to a major loss of confidence in the political and economic system that has created and maintained the deception, the fallacy of infinite growth on a finite planet.

Each human group was weighed more heavily by one emergency than another. And, up to that moment, each group was looking for its own liberation, its own rebalancing. And, while each story was being told, each group suffered the effects of its imbalance, considering that it was the most important.

At first, the war did not help to structure the different struggles for liberation. Later, under the impact of disbelief and the paralyzing effects of the war, everyone became more and more entrenched. Every organization, collective, movement was dramatizing its cause to find support, but the people in their own faith had the strength to survive in the scarcity and perplexity in the face of so many serious emergencies.

Years ago, the movement of the "Indignats" had filled the streets with youth encampments that showed the new generation's rejection of the failures of democracy and the speculative economy. The experience, beyond the controversial electoral impact, showed the power of cooperating in the organization of protest and in generating new ways of gathering and deciding.

Also, years ago the movement for independence had channeled in national and local organizations the capacity for mass mobilization and to carry out large punctual actions, especially of denunciation and some of civil disobedience, such as the repressed referendum of October, 1st 2017.

In both cases, the model of mobilization and organization had shown great strengths, but also some weaknesses. Both models were framed in the traditional and mythical "revolutionary" model that books and movies had spread and extolled as the "only" model of change, usually successful thanks to the use of revolutionary violence.

The "D" day of the "R" Revolution fails if the dreamed objective is not achieved.

- If after occupying streets for a few weeks there is no change of regime, political and economic structures...
- If after a massive and distributed act of voting that is strongly repressed, independence is not achieved...

And so we learned that what had failed was neither the actions nor the movements but the creation of a fantasy model, an expectation of what revolution meant.

One of the attempts to rethink the prevailing theory of change - if you make the revolution everything will change in a day - was the manifesto "Global nonviolent re-evolution or total extermination" (see message 46).

The change of model, of the theory of change to be applied, came about as a result of several apparently fortuitous and unconnected events:

a. Reflection on the 50th anniversary of the first alternative civilian service of the concientious objectors to the military service in Can Serra 1975-2025 and the nonviolent strategy followed to end the conscription.
b. The insufficiency of large mobilizations in public space to achieve the objectives of any movement in a framework of formal democracy (Indignats 15M; Moviment per la independència...).
c. The contributions of the youth meeting *"Sobremesa"* in the summer of 2022 focused on the fact that trust is the basis of cooperation.
d. The challenges of the Engler brothers *(This is un uprising)* on the need to create new theories of change from the existing ones, usually opposed, we achieve the desired change when: 1. we cultivate personal transformation; 2. we launch mass protests; 3. we equip ourselves with a powerful and influential organization; 4. we create alternatives to the system we criticize; and, 5. we have an impact from public institutions.
e. Reading *Unstoppable Us* (Yuval Harari) and his vision that Homo Sapiens have dominated the earth - and extinguished most species - thanks to the ability to create

stories or myths that help us cooperate to face incredible challenges.

We will now break down the influence of these different facts that will allow us to generate another theory of change that will help to cooperate to face the emergency states.

a. **The strength of the movement of objectors to the conscription** was based on the public refusal to do compulsory military service and to freely assume the corresponding imprisonment. But also, for some years, in the creation by the objectors of alternative civilian services to serve the needs of specific neighborhoods. Local groups that showed a link to the territory to confront the aggressions and imbalances that affected it. "Global action, local action".

b. **Heirs of the anti-Francoist mass struggles**, the vindication of any right had the inertia of calling for demonstrations, rallies and strikes, for a few hours or days. In a regime where the right to demonstrate, to assemble and to strike (not a general strike) were recognized, these actions were insufficient to modify the correlation of forces based on the economic and political interests of the elites or on constitutional systems that were almost immutable when these interests were touched.

They realized that these types of street mobilizations, integrated into formal democracies, were not a pillar of power and, therefore, were less and less effective in achieving the changes that were being proposed. To the point that only if there were riots, where the police intervened to repress them –or to provoke them and thus have justification to repress them–, these events became news. However, even so, they did not always have the effects expected by the organizers; sometimes the effects were the opposite, when a part of society was against them because they saw public order threatened.

c. **The week-long "Sobremesa" meeting** of 500 young people from more than 100 collectives showed that there was a new wisdom in both the objectives and the methods of social transformation:

- Only the individual change of values, of behaviors, does not always provoke in time the general change, especially if it has to be done to face an emergency.
- In order to motivate people to take part in a collective action, it is necessary to identify what are the common roots of the different emergencies, to share a story about the causes and where we want to go in order to find solutions.
- Events - more or less manipulated by those who control

and contain them - often cause us to react, but to understand them, it is necessary to place them in context, and in trends over time, and to discover the structures that provoke or sustain them.

- Discovering the paradigm that gives change meaning will help us to better focus on what to do and how to do it. "Trust leads to cooperation. Jealousy leads to mutual destruction."
- When a human group weaves a narrative that motivates and unites it, makes its values and practices explicit, creates its language and its signs and symbols it will facilitate internal and external communication.

d. They realized that there is necessary **integration and complementarity of the different theories of change**, too often opposed among the different actors of a movement, in order to generate a new one in each context and with the people and organizations involved: if I do not participate in the change of mentality, values and practices, I cannot contribute much to the organization or entity that wants these changes, whether through more or less risky actions or by participating in spaces where the desired change begins to live. With this force we can press from the outside or from within the institutional changes necessary for the desired change to take on the scope of a legal framework that validates it.

e. **Why do some stories fit and stretch and others do not?** Because of the explanatory force of complexity? By the more or less coercive imposition? Why are we asked to transcend our individual smallness or our temporal futility? Why do they make us participants of a great adventure, of an incredible challenge, of a historical moment?

This incredible story that will take us to the "V" day, began discreetly when a small group of neighbors, one day checked the pace of life they were leading, and asked themselves:

- What can we do to face the emergencies we are experiencing?

  Q One said – Nothing. Everything is too big, so we can do nothing.
  (Don't be defeatist! If it were so, why don't you kill yourself)

  Q Another said - Vote. If we vote with conscience, our representatives will fix things.
  (Oh, come on, the others said, corruption stops everything.... parties don't count anymore; they don't represent us)

  Q And a third one exclaimed: - what is needed is to participate in an entity that works to stop aggressions.

(Dear, I don't have time, working with jobs all day I can't even make ends meet)

Q And another one murmured: - we have no choice but to pray, humans are selfish and none of them will save us. (So now you can wait, it's better if you wait for a miracle)

Q Stop being complacent, what we need is to start living the world we want, to change our habits, our shops, to stop maintaining with our money this evil world... (Ugh, to much work and problems, I don't want to lose the wellbeing I have now...)

• After the break, once again after so many others, there was a silence, long and deep. The situation was too serious to face it with one more conversation. What kind of world were they leaving to their children, and grandchildren...? The world was very big. The country too. But the region, the town, the neighborhood, the street, the houses... they were close, if they didn't take care of them, who would?

• And they asked again, what can we do to face the emergencies we are experiencing, here, in our environment, what imbalances do we suffer or provoke, what aggressions do we receive or exert? And they started to make a list:

- People without work, without a home, who live in bad conditions, who squat spaces in order to have a shelter...
- The factory that underpays the workers and pollutes the river and the air
- The farms that mistreat the animals and that drain the water from the wells and springs.
- The Polices quarters that continues to be a bastion that is backward highborne.
- The male chauvinism that continues to threaten women and even assaults some of them.
- And other more general aggressions such as climate change, banking extortions or war...

- And now let's say for each one of us which aggression is the most serious, the most urgent and the easiest to deal with? They were sharing, unravelling, prioritizing. Some of themthey knew very well, and those they didn't, they decided to give themselves a few days to learn more things.

- They agreed to start by making a campaign about the easiest aggression to stop. If they succeeded, they would have more strength to take on another one.

- "And how to organize the campaign?" A couple of them said they had taken a course or read about **nonviolent struggle...** (see message 50)

- "And how do we organize ourselves? How can we avoid repeating the usual vices of organizations?" They were also inspired by new models, such as the **sociocracy** (see message 54).

- "And, if necessary, how can we coordinate with other groups so that we can be stronger and stronger without creating the problems of large organizations?" "Hey, stop the cart. When it is the case, we will talk about it!"

And so it was that a small group, with a clear and achievable objective, managed to attack a local aggression and took the initiative to attack other local aggressions or to coordinate with other groups from other neighboring areas... (and in this, they were also inspired by the model of sociocracy).

They realized that small, almost imperceptible changes could provoke great changes... unimaginable metamorphoses.

And that small, well-organized and coordinated groups can have a lot of strength, without needing charismatic leaders... who, if they did, could jeopardize the whole organization.

They realized that they were writing a story that could be read and replicated everywhere.

And that, in fact, they began to feel part of a nonviolent liberation army against a system that attacked people and their territories and that, when the moment of repression or occupation came, they would be well prepared to confront it with an effective **civil, citizen, nonviolent self-defense.**

The "V" day, the day of "D" of Truth, because the different conditions had led to it, because they had reached the objective by making an effort in the coherent means. That's why it was the "V" day of Truth, because it made them understand that the "D" days until now had often been fables or lies, that they had generated great frustrations in making people believe that the revolution had triumphed that day and that, because the situation has been inverted, everything would be different, liberated from the executioners, from fear and from all constriction...

By an Anonymus - XXI century

Annex.
Complementary transformation routes

A. Are we aware of the different ways of transformation?

Usually, in any conversation about how to approach the solution of a social, political, economic, environmental problem... we can identify different ways of transformation, or as they say, different "theories of change" that we usually oppose: "what we need to do is to go out to the streets...", or ! only if we educate...", or "if we don't change, nothing can change..." #ADNcat

B. How to make the different ways of transformation complementary?

We can say, according to Paul Engler, that these ways are: personal change, education, mobilization, organization, institutional policy and the creation of alternatives. If we make them conscious, we can make them complementary. Let's apply them now to "how to stop wars" with concrete examples from our own home. #ADNcat

C. Personal change

Introspection helps us to become aware of the impulses, emotions, feelings, thoughts that provoke more or less violent, covetous, passive, compromised, pacifying behaviors... Cultivating nonviolent attitudes will allow us to face conflicts without increasing the spiral of violence and hatred in relationships of all kinds. With violent or male chauvinist attitudes we can contribute little to peace building or feminism.

The ultimate test of the change of vision or attitude is the change in our social practices: change in consumption, work, housing, investment, food, mobility, energy...; in voting, social and political commitment, in the payment of taxes... All these conscious changes can favor the culture of war or the culture of peace, they can reduce aggressions and cultural and structural violence... or they can increase them. #ADNcat

D. Education

Education can be the magic word that some believe will fix in future generations what we do not know how to fix ourselves. We must learn more by imitation and emulation than by speeches, especially when these are not consistent with the behavior of those who preach them.

Education for peace encompasses a wide range of visions, education, training... for all ages, with the aim of reducing violent relationships, transforming conflicts and combating war and its causes. Among the references (in Catalonia): Edualter, Unipau, Justícia i Pau, Escola Cultura de Pau, Servei Civil Internacional, Fundació Carta de la pau dirigida a l'ONU, Lluita noviolenta, l'Escola de formació Guillem Agulló #ADNcat

https://edualter.org/ca
https://www.unipau.org/
https://www.justiciaipau.org/
https://escolapau.uab.cat/ca/inicio/

https://www.scicat.org/
https://cartadelapau.org/pau-possible/
https://www.lluitanoviolenta.cat/
https://escolaguillemagullo.cat/

E. The mobilization

At different times there have been great social movements against war and in favor of peace. Among the most relevant in recent years in Catalonia have been www.aturemlaguerra.org and

"Casa nostra casa vostra". But we can also consider others that denounce violence against women, for those without a home, for housing and decent work, the right to decide... #ADNcat

F. The organization

One thing are campaigns or occasional mobilizations, and the other are organizations that seek transformation from well-equipped structures, with permanent support, with international projection. In general, these organizations can be found at www.lafede.cat and, in particular, within the peace and non-violence axis. Some of them are oriented to denounce different elements of the war or armament conflicts: Centre Delàs, Fundipau, Novact . #ADNcat

G. Institutional policy (in Catalonia)

What emerges from the citizenry, from social movements, sometimes has institutional resonance, either because some parties incorporate values and demands into their programs, or because parliaments or governments create policies aimed in this case at peace and conflict. The Llei de foment de la pau (Law of promotion of Peace), and it's outcome : Consell català de foment de la pau, and, more operationally, the Institut Català Internacional per la Pau, are examples. #ADNcat

http://sac.gencat.cat/sacgencat/AppJava/organisme_fitxa.jsp?codi=13572
https://www.icip.cat/ca/

H. The creation of alternatives

In this case, the Civilian System of Nonviolent Defense project aims to contribute to lay the foundations of a **Civilian System of Nonviolent Defense *as an alternative*** to the usual **Military Systems of Violent Defense**. If it obtains the necessary contribution and citizen involvement, it wants to propose how this Civil Nonviolent Defense System could be in Catalonia, both in the current phase and in the case of the emergence of an independent state. #ADNcat

https://lluitanoviolenta.cat/projecte-defensa-noviolenta

Nonviolent Self-Defense (#ADNcat) in 100 messages and an incredible story
Martí Olivella Solé

AutoDefensa Noviolenta (#ADNcat) en 100 mensajes y una historia increíble
Martí Olivella Solé

AutoDefensa Noviolenta (#ADNcat) en 100 missatges i una història increïble
Martí Olivella Solé

MONTABER Brutau, 160 – 08203 Sabadell (Barcelona) – Tel. +34-931 429 486 – montaber@montaber.es – www.montaber.es

9 788419 109606